# INTERESTING STORIES FOR CURIOUS PEOPLE

*A Collection of Fascinating Stories Relating to History, Science, Pop Culture, and Just about Anything Else You Can Think Of*

**BILL O'NEILL**

ISBN: 978-1-64845-044-0

# DON'T FORGET YOUR FREE BOOKS

# Contents

# Introduction

Welcome to *Interesting Stories for Curious People: A Fascinating Collection of Stories Relating to History, Pop Culture, Science, and Just About Anything Else You Can Think Of.* This book will introduce you to some of the strangest facts on the face of the earth. You'll learn about a Kansas town that people claim is so haunted that many call it the "Gateway to Hell," as well as an urban myth about a Soviet drilling expedition that may—or may not have—opened a portal to Hell.

You'll learn about strange historical facts that were more than likely overlooked in your history classes. How Alexander the Great died, how Cleopatra died, what happened to American Indian leader Sequoya, and the truth about Christopher Columbus' expedition are just a few of the historical stories you'll read about.

The thin line between science fact and science fiction is also explored in many stories. You'll read about a star that is many times bigger and brighter than our own, what will happen when computers become self-aware, what causes "brain freeze," and how the government has been actively searching for extraterrestrials.

You'll also learn a few pop culture tidbits that you may find interesting. Did you know that several popular American 1970s sitcoms were inspired by shows on British television? You'll read about how the popular 1960s American sitcom

1

*Hogan's Heroes* was hated by some but loved by many and how the star of the show lived a dark, double life. And you'll find out about how A-list actor Mark Wahlberg was once a drug-dealing thug before he became one of the highest paid entertainers in the world.

There are also a number of true crime cases thrown in this book for good measure. But these true crime stories are among some of the strangest you'll have ever heard about. We have a celebrity cannibal, serial killers, and a young antihero who liked to steal planes in his bare feet. Undoubtedly, these anecdotes will keep you glued to the pages.

And for all you sports fans, there are plenty of interesting stories about some of your favorite athletes and games.

Prepare to laugh, shrug, shake your head, and learn tons of new, intriguing information. Who says reading can't be fun?!

# Fighting Boredom
# in the Ancient World

With everything that the modern world has to offer (from the Internet to television and numerous sports-related pastimes), we really have no reason to experience boredom. But of course it still happens. Maybe we are victims of sensory overload or perhaps we've just become spoiled from all the technology at our disposal.

Have you ever wondered what people did to pass the time when the Giza pyramids were being built?

Life may have been tougher in ancient Egypt, and people didn't live as long on average, but they still had to devise ways to deal with their boredom. After all, it was not "all work and no play for Neferhotep."

You may be surprised to know that the ancient Egyptians enjoyed imbibing beer nearly every day, oftentimes all day! It wasn't that the Egyptians were necessarily a culture of soaks, they just didn't have access to potable water. Even back then, the Nile River was full of animal waste, making it undrinkable for the most part. Beer was the safe alternative.

While the majority of Egyptians drank beer, the nobles chose wine as their favored alcoholic beverage.

All Egyptians enjoyed public and private celebrations, where a certain level of drunkenness was not only expected, but encouraged. As they were drinking their beer or wine, many Egyptians also enjoyed playing the world's oldest board game—*senet*. Although modern scholars don't know all the details of game play, senet was a two-player game where pieces were moved after rolling dice, similar to backgammon. Senet games probably got pretty heated when the players were drunk, especially since betting would have been frequent.

So, the next time your power goes out and you're feeling bored, think about the ancient Egyptians.

# E.T. Are You out There?

Recent polls show that about half of all people believe in extraterrestrial (alien) life, so there's a good chance that you are one of those people. It seems logical to believers that with all of the stars and planets out there, at least one of them has to have life.

…and then there are all those people who claim to have seen an actual UFO.

Polls show that 10 to 20 percent of all people claim to have seen something floating around the sky that simply could not be explained. All of this lends to the idea that aliens have been visiting (and possibly making contact with us) for some time.

But what if we've been the ones making contact?

Of course, we don't yet have the technology to send out our own manned space probes beyond the solar system, but, like E.T. did in the movie, we do have the ability to send and receive long-distance messages.

The Search for Extraterrestrial Intelligence (SETI) generally refers to a variety of different programs intended to discover alien life through airwaves. In the decades since World War II, various individuals, universities, and eventually even NASA have developed programs to study radio waves coming from space to see if any of them have been sent by intelligent life.

There are also programs where messages have been sent from

Earth to beyond the solar system, which are known as "active SETI."

This may sound like a pretty straightforward way of contacting aliens, but it is a lot more complex than it sounds. Any "message" received or sent would be contained inside radio waves, therefore making it difficult to determine if there is an actual message present. It would be up to the SETI scientists to peel off the layers of waves to see if there is a message hidden within. In other words, we may have already received alien communication without realizing it!

There is also the fact that any aliens out there might be at our level of technological advancement, or even behind us.

And finally, our messages may have been received by some beings who just don't care.

Would you respond to one of our messages?

# Ptolemy and the Flat Earth

Why did Columbus have such a difficult time acquiring funding for his expeditions to Asia? Most people would probably say: "Because everyone thought that the world was flat." Chances are, you were probably taught this in grade school and the idea just persisted into adulthood.

I know this because I, too, was taught this as a kid.

Unfortunately, it is just another lie we were all told.

It's not that this lie is maliciously retold or is part of some conspiracy theory, but it is a lie none the less.

It is true that, for most of our existence, humans have believed the Earth was flat. But by the fifth century BC that view began to be challenged. A wave of scientific inquiry and rationalism infused Greece during that period, especially in the city of Athens, leading many learned men to come to the conclusion that the Earth was shaped like the celestial objects.

During the second century AD, the Greek scientist Ptolemy produced the first map that showed the world as a sphere rather than a flat disc. Although Ptolemy's map was missing the Americas and Australia, it was the first to include longitude and latitude. Furthermore, he accurately calculated that there were other unknown continents—*terra incognita*.

Knowledge of Ptolemy's maps lapsed during the Dark Ages in Europe but resurfaced in the early fifteenth century during the Renaissance. It was during the Renaissance that the maps were translated from their original Greek into Latin which, although a dead language, was one that most educated Western Europeans of the time could read.

The Renaissance happened to coincide with the Age of Exploration.

By the time Christopher Columbus made his first voyage to the Americas in 1492, knowledge of Ptolemy's maps was well-known among the nobles and explorers of Europe. Benefit-to-cost analyses are what actually kept Columbus from getting funding from the Portuguese and English; they simply believed that an expedition to Asia across the Atlantic would cost more than any type of profit it could net.

But sea monsters? Well, that's another story!

# All That Bee Buzzing

If you're about forty-five or older, you probably remember hearing during the 1970s about how "killer bees" were making their way north and would be taking over the United States by the 1990s. It was actually quite a scare. There were numerous documentaries filmed about it and several movies were produced—most notably the 1978 Irwin Allen film, *The Swarm*.

Obviously, the killer bee menace never destroyed America.

So, why were people so scared of these killer bees? And have they even lived up to the name?

To begin with, the term "killer bee" is actually just a colloquialism for a new type of bee that was bred by Brazilian biologist Warwick Kerr in the 1950s. Kerr crossed European bees with East African bees to create a new "Africanized" hybrid that would create more honey. But these bees were quickly found to be difficult to control. They escaped from their controlled environments in 1956 and quickly spread across Brazil.

Within a few short years, the Africanized bees had spread through much of Latin America, especially the tropical and subtropical zones.

The Africanized bees soon proved to be much more aggressive than normal bees and they had a unique ability to migrate long distances. Wherever the Africanized bees went, they often replaced the normal bee populations.

But have they earned a reputation as killer bees?

The sting of an Africanized bee is no more toxic than that of a normal bee. But Africanized bees are more aggressive, attack in swarms, and have been known to chase people for nearly a mile. It is believed that at least one thousand people have been killed by Africanized bees worldwide since the 1950s, which isn't that many when you put it into perspective. By contrast, over seven hundred thousand people are killed *each year* by mosquitos, and about one hundred are killed by elephants.

Still, you certainly don't want to get attacked by Africanized bees. The elderly and the sick tend to have the highest fatality rates from killer bee attacks, as well as apiarists (professional beekeepers). Experts say that the biggest threat Africanized bees pose to America is in apiculture. The killer bees' European lineage has allowed them to migrate farther north than a true East African bee would be able to do, but the long winters of the Midwest, Northwest, and Northeast appear to be an effective barrier.

It looks like all the doomsday predictions about a killer bee invasion of the United States will never happen. I guess that means *The Swarm II* won't be hitting theaters anytime soon.

# I Know I've Been Here Before

We've all had it happen to us at least once in our lives: we sit down to eat in a restaurant where we've never been, and suddenly we get that feeling that we've been there before. Sometimes we even know where certain things are. How uncanny!

Of course, that feeling is called *déjà vu*, which translates from French into English as "already seen."

Since this phenomenon is so widespread among the human population, scientists have tried (and failed) to determine its origins. Researchers have determined that some medical conditions, such as epilepsy, can create the feeling of déjà vu in some people. But this still doesn't explain why the majority of healthy people have had this experience at least once in their lives.

Some research points toward dreams as being the culprit in some cases, while other studies suggest that some people build false memories based on new experiences. Illicit drug use has also been said to be a reason behind déjà vu.

Still, these scientific explanations don't explain the majority of cases of déjà vu. So what are some other explanations?

Psychologists who are followers of Carl Jung argue that déjà vu is simply a case of the always present, but usually dormant, collective unconscious coming to surface. They argue that, though you personally may have never been in that restaurant before, we are all connected to the collective unconscious, and you are therefore experiencing a shared memory. Jungians further believe that the closer you are to other individuals the more connected you are. Therefore, if one of your living blood relatives sat in that restaurant, or even an ancestor, it could result in a stronger sense of déjà vu.

Yes, I know, pretty deep stuff. But there is still another potential explanation for déjà vu—the supernatural.

Some people believe that déjà vu comes from an experience you've actually had in a past life. Of course, this explanation is more popular in many Asian countries where beliefs in reincarnation are more popular than in the West. This may also explain why understanding déjà vu is much less of an obsession in Asia.

Finally, there are those who think déjà vu is the result of possession. Yes, that's right, this theory holds that evil spirits who were once human have found a way to enter your body, which gives you that feeling that you've been somewhere before.

In the end, there are a few things that we can say definitively about déjà vu. One, its origins will probably never be known for certain. Two, if you've had that feeling before, chances are you'll feel it again.

In fact, you may even feel like you've read this before. Have you?

# The Hole into Hell

Urban legends are a lot of fun to share when you sit around a table with your friends and family. There's the one that says gang members purposely drive around with their headlights off at night as part of a gang initiation. When an unsuspecting do-gooder flashes his or her headlights to let the gang members know theirs are off, the criminals turn around and kill the driver.

Another urban myth, which was common in the 1960s, involved a woman who really loved her beehive haircut. She loved it so much that she never washed it. At some point, a spider decided to make a nest in her hair and eventually gave birth to a whole brood of spider babies.

A bit gross and, for the most part, a totally unbelievable story. And as probable as the gangbangers with the headlights off may sound, there are no documented cases.

But have you ever heard the urban legend about the Russian hole into hell?

According to this tale, a Soviet/Russian mining operation in Siberia was drilling the deepest humans had ever gone. Once they reached a depth of about nine miles, they hit a cavity that was more than 2,000°F. For whatever reason, the team sent some heat-resistant microphones into the cavity and recorded what sounded like screams of agony.

And so, the legend of the Russian hole into hell was born.

The supposed sounds of hell were played on a 1989 American religious broadcast, and by the late 1990s the Internet had brought the urban legend to all corners of the globe. There's a good chance that you heard the recording in the late 1990s or early 2000s. I did, and it did seem pretty creepy. But it was all a big hoax.

The precise origin of the hoax remains a mystery, although the sounds were later determined to have come from a 1972 horror film titled *Baron of Blood*.

Like all urban legends, though, there is probably a kernel of truth to this story. In 1989, the Soviet Union conducted a project called the Kola Superdeep Borehole where they bored nearly eight miles into the earth. The project never made it to hell or dredged up any demons, but it is the deepest vertical borehole on record. I guess they'll have to dig a little deeper to make it to hell.

# How Did Superman Die?

Sometime between 1:30 a.m. and 2:00 a.m. on June 16, 1959, Superman was shot in the head and killed in his Los Angeles home. It wasn't really Superman, of course, but George Reeves—the man who played him in the popular 1950s television series. His death was ruled a suicide, but there were (and still are) many who doubt that finding.

Reeves was only forty-five, had a beautiful fiancé, and had built a reputable and lucrative career in Hollywood.

But beneath the surface there were problems.

There were reports that Reeves was drinking too much and suffering from depression over the direction of his career: He felt he had been typecast as Superman and it was hurting his chances at other roles. Also, *The Adventures of Superman* was cancelled in 1958, which ended Reeves' sturdy source of income.

According to the official police report, Reeves had company on the evening of June 15. At some point during the night, he left his guests and went upstairs to bed. He came downstairs a little while later, complaining that the party was too loud. Then he had a drink with his company before going back upstairs. The guests heard a single gunshot a short time after that.

It seemed like a cut-and-dried case of suicide until some inconsistencies came to the surface. Reeve's fiancé, Leonore

Lemmon, reportedly came running down the stairs after the gunshot sounded and asked the guests to say she had been downstairs the entire time. Then, there was the fact that there were no fingerprints on the gun and no gunpowder residue on Reeve's hands. As the decades passed, a number of alternate theories began to take root.

One theory was that Lemmon either killed Reeves in a fit of passion or by accident. The accidental shooting theory has some credence because two other rounds fired from the gun that killed Reeves were found embedded in his bedroom floor, yet his guests only heard one shot. The gun may have discharged in previous arguments between Lemmon and Reeves, but this final time proved fatal. The reason why Lemmon and Reeves may have been fighting is related to another alternate theory.

It was rumored that Reeves was having an affair with Toni Mannix, who was the wife of MGM vice president Eddie Mannix. The latter was reputed to be an extremely jealous man who had mob ties. So, the theory goes, Mannix called in some favors and had Reeves killed.

The alternate theories were good enough to inspire an episode on the popular television show *Unsolved Mysteries*. The 2006 film *Hollywoodland*, starring Ben Affleck, also explored the possibilities surrounding the actor's death. But unfortunately, since everyone involved with the case is now deceased, the complete truth will probably never be known.

The secrets of Superman's death died with him, and possibly his killer.

# It's Hotdish Not Casserole

If you've ever been to Minnesota, you probably noticed that the people are fairly nice but a little bit quirky. After all, besides being the "Land of 10,000 Lakes," it happens to be the home of Garrison Keillor and the setting for the surreal film *Fargo*. It is also a place where people like to fish on frozen lakes in the middle of the winter. What's more, the residents elected a former professional wrestler to be their governor. So maybe it goes without saying that Minnesotans have their own unique cuisine.

Minnesotans enjoy eating walleye—baked, grilled, or fried, although grilled is best—along with a side of wild rice, and they wash it down with a Premium Grain Belt beer or some pop—it's pop in Minnesota, not soda!

Another favorite dish in Minnesota is "hotdish," but if you've never been to that state you might be wondering what it is.

Well, hotdish is simply any casserole, but in Minnesota they take the dish to a whole different level. Many different types of hotdishes reflect Minnesota's Scandinavian and German ethnic background, although other types, such as Pizza Hotdish and Mexican Hotdish, demonstrate Minnesotans' ability to accommodate more modern tastes. Hotdishes are quite easy to make; they are served as daily meals and as dishes for larger gatherings. The Minnesota U.S. congressional delegation has even held their own hotdish-making competitions!

The origins of the term definitely come from the farmlands of the state and probably are related to its Scandinavian background. One thing's for sure, if you spend enough time in Minnesota, you should find a hotdish you like, you betcha!

# Not Your Average Flag

You might think that once you've seen one flag you've seen them all, at least when it comes to their shape. After all, all national flags are rectangular, right? That's true for all national flags except one—Nepal.

Yes, Nepal's national flag has the unique distinction of being the world's only non-quadrilateral national flag. It has the shape of two pennants, one on top of the other, and is red with a blue outline. It features a white moon on the top pennant and a white sun on the bottom pennant.

This flag replaced a more traditional flag in 1962 and has since been the subject of a lot of discussion (obviously, as we are talking about it here), bringing a certain degree of notoriety to the small country otherwise known as the birthplace of Buddha and a destination for mountain climbing and hash enthusiasts from around the world.

Sometimes referred to as the "Triangle Flag," the two pennants of the Nepali flag are said to represent the two dominant religions of the country, Hinduism and Buddhism, and their ability to coexist peacefully side by side.

Since the flag is so unique, it has caused minor diplomatic incidents on occasion. During the 2016 Summer Olympic Games in Rio de Janeiro, Brazil, the Nepali flag was produced with larger white areas to make it proportionately similar to other flags. Although the majority of the world didn't notice the change and Nepal's leaders didn't care, some Nepalis took to social media to voice their displeasure. The flag furor quickly died down and the people of Nepal soon went back to their daily lives.

Although new countries are formed every year in the world, it looks like Nepal will continue to hold the distinction of having the world's only non-rectangular national flag for the foreseeable future.

# I Have Brain Freeze, Bro

It's happened to all of us. It's a hot day, usually in the middle of the summer, and you want to cool off with some tasty ice cream or a Popsicle. You take a couple of bites and then it hits you! That sharp painful sensation that begins behind your eyes and quickly spreads to the rest of your head. It sucks. It really, really sucks. But at least the sensation usually leaves almost as quickly as it comes.

Of course, I'm talking about what most people know as "brain freeze." Scientists identify it as a stimulus headache, or *sphenopalatine ganglioneuralgia* for all you science nerds. You may be surprised to learn that serious studies have been conducted on brain freeze at major institutions such as Harvard University.

These studies have shown that brain freeze happens when an extremely cold substance quickly hits the roof of the mouth, causing the capillaries to constrict, followed by an equally quick rewarming when warm air is reintroduced to the mouth. This warming causes vasodilation, or a widening of the blood vessels. The rapid changes in temperature in the upper mouth lead to this painful sensation.

Most of this is standard knowledge, but a study by Dr. Jorge Serrador revealed that there is a correlation between brain freeze and migraine sufferers. His research found that those suffering from migraines are more likely to get brain freeze, which suggests that there may be similar biological processes at work. Understanding how the contraction and widening of blood vessels in the brain take place may help scientists develop better headache medicines.

But what do we do about brain freeze right now?

Well, that's easy enough. Slow down when you're eating ice cream, or if you are unfortunate enough to get hit with a case of brain freeze, put your tongue on the top of your mouth. It works every time.

# Lay Down Your Head,
# Tom Dooley

Deep in the North Carolina Appalachians, the people believe passionately in a sense of justice and they also like to tell some stories. Both are perhaps a result of the people's Scotch-Irish ancestry, and if you've ever traveled to these parts, you know what I mean. The locals like to tell legendary tales of moonshiners, bootleggers, and unrepentant Confederate soldiers who lived above the law and often paid for it with their lives. Many of these legends have been turned into songs, creating a genre known as "murder ballads."

Chances are, you've heard one of these ballads: the 1958 hit "Tom Dooley" by the Kingston Trio.

If haven't heard the song, it is actually quite dark and depressing for an otherwise optimistic era in American history. The song relates how a young man named Tom Dooley came back home to North Carolina from the Civil War and got involved in a love triangle. He killed the woman he was cheating on his girlfriend with, was caught for the crime, and hanged after a trial. The Kingston Trio's song was taken directly from the local legends.

But the local legends were based on facts.

The real Tom Dooley was a man named Tom Dula who was born in Wilkes County, North Carolina in the heart of the

Appalachian Mountains in 1845. Due to the people's accent in that part of Appalachia, Dula's last name was pronounced with a long "e" sound.

Dula was quite the player with the ladies around the county when he was a young man, getting involved in an on-again, off-again relationship with a girl named Anne Foster and, later, two of her cousins, Laura and Pauline Foster. He was said to be a skilled musician and very articulate and literate for a backwoodsman with little formal education.

But Tom Dula's carefree life had to be put on hold when he went to fight for the Confederacy.

Anne Foster had married a man named James Melton before the war, but as fate would have it, both Dula and Melton were captured by Union forces and spent time in the same military prison. Both men returned to Wilkes County, which is when things got interesting.

And a bit confusing.

Melton returned to his wife Anne, but Dula continued to see her, as well as Laura and Pauline. Eventually, Laura went missing and was later discovered dead, and Dula was on the run. When Dula was captured a short time later in another county, his guilt sure looked certain to most people. Even after his trial was moved to another county, he was still convicted and hanged from the end of a rope.

But the reality is that there was no physical evidence tying him to the murder, and there were other reasonable suspects.

The ballad contends that Laura was pregnant when she died, which means that the list of possible suspects of her murder is lengthy. The prosecution argued that Dula killed Laura to cover up his indiscretion so that he could continue his freewheeling lifestyle. But Anne was a potential suspect due to jealousy; she also made incriminating statements to family members. The ballad mentions a man named "Grayson" as a jealous rival or perhaps one of the many men Dula cuckolded in his short life. Perhaps the murderer was one of these men?

Tom Dula proclaimed his innocence until the very end.

# Why Not Just Call It
# a Waiting Room?

At some point in your life you've probably watched a talk show, daytime or late night, and heard one of the guests talk about something he or she did in the "green room." The first time you heard it you were probably a little confused, but after a few minutes you figured out that it simply refers to a waiting room. It turns out that this is a pretty standard term in the entertainment industry that's used around the world in all forms of media, not just television. You might think that the term is some sort of artsy way of making something sound cooler than it really is, but the reality is no one is quite sure how the term originated.

Theater historians have been able to determine that the term was first used in the entertainment industry during the European Renaissance, but they are unsure of its original, precise meaning. Some think that it originated from the area where actors practiced their craft, known as "The Green," while others think it had to do with the color of early theaters. By the early twentieth century, though, it had become a common term in theater for the area where actors waited before entering for their scenes.

There may be a scientific reason for the green room.

Although most modern green rooms are rarely painted green, psychologists have identified green as a color that produces calming, soothing effects in people. Numerous studies have shown that the color green helps alleviate anxiety and nervousness and that it tends to be one of the most positive colors.

Obviously, people weren't conducting in-depth psychological experiments during the Renaissance like they do today. But perhaps these early directors realized that their actors were more relaxed when they entered the stage from a green-colored room.

So the next time you hear someone talk about being in a "green room," consider the possibility that just saying the name of the color might help them relax.

# The British Archie Bunker

The 1970s American sitcom *All in the Family* remains one of the most popular and enduring shows in American history. It is nearly always in rotation on some network, and practically every American over the age of twenty is familiar with the offensive, yet lovable character Archie Bunker and his many catchphrases, including: "stifle," "ding bat," and, of course, "meat head."

*All in the Family* was centered on the middle-aged, conservative, working-class Archie Bunker as he lived his life in the Astoria neighborhood of Queens, New York. Alongside him were his genuine, yet dense wife, Edith, his hippie son-in-law Mike, and his daughter Gloria. There was also a range of supporting actors who were often foils to Archie and challenged his beliefs. Though the show tackled many controversial issues in America during the 1970s, it actually got its inspiration from across the pond.

From 1965 to 1975, British television audiences tuned in each week to watch main character Alfred Garnett offend his family and British society in *Till Death Us Do Part*. This show followed the same formula as *All in the Family*: Alfred tackled the issues of the day in the most offensive ways possible, but he also became a fan favorite due to his authentic nature. He was supported by his wife Elise, his daughter Rita, and her communist husband Mike.

An American television producer saw the show and knew that it could be a hit if it was slightly modified for an American audience. The Bunkers were made into a solidly middle-class family, and the relationship between Archie and Edith was less antagonistic than it was with their British counterparts. American Mike was made far less radical, and the Bunkers were given a more diverse range of neighbors. For instance, the Jeffersons were the first black family in the Bunker's neighborhood.

The formula worked so well that Norman Lear, and then other American producers, decided to replicate it with other shows.

The 1970s hit *Sanford and Son* was actually based on the 1960s British sitcom *Steptoe and Son*. Although the location of the show, as well as the race of the main characters, was changed, the premise remained the same—a curmudgeonly and often verbally abusive father operated a junk yard with his long-suffering son.

One of the least known (and most interesting) of all American sitcoms that got its inspiration in England was *Three's Company*. That's right, the 1970s-80s silly sitcom about a playboy and his two female roommates, with whom he maintained a platonic relationship, was based on the 1970s British sitcom *Man About the House.* The most interesting part about the *Three's Company/Man About the House* connection is that the latter show produced two spin-offs that were directly copied by its American counterpart. In *Man about the House,* the trio's landlords left the show for their own show, titled *George and Mildred*; on *Three's Company* the same situation took place, producing *The Ropers.* Finally, when *Man About the House* ended, Robin Tripp, the primary male character, left the apartment to live with his girlfriend Vicky. On *Three's*

*Company*, Jack Tripper left the apartment to move in with his girlfriend Vicky on the show *Three's a Crowd*.

It sure seems like being a writer for one of these shows would've been an easy gig. You would've just had to get a hold of the British scripts, change some names and locations, and then apparently you'd have a hit show.

# November 15, 1915

When it comes to important dates in world history, November 15, 1915 doesn't particularly stand out to most. For some, however, this day marked the occurrence of a strange, unexplainable event.

At least, according to legend.

By this time, Europe had been embroiled in a war for nearly a year and a half on three fronts. The Western Front had devolved to vicious trench fighting and the occasional use of chemical weapons, the Eastern Front was ebbing and flowing, and the Austrians and Italians were fighting the cold temperatures and altitude, as much as each other, on the Southern Front. The casualties were mounting for all sides when this strange incident supposedly happened.

At 10:30 p.m., as men on all fronts were fighting, hundreds in different locations, from both sides, just laid down their arms. The legend states that all of the men who quit fighting claimed to have seen a bright light in the sky, and then they just lost control of their bodies.

Again, this is a legend, which means that it may or may not be true—or there may be a grain of truth to it. There are not any official government records known to exist that mention the mysterious light, although the chance that any government official would have documented something like that in 1915 is unlikely due to the pressures of war and it just sounding "crazy."

Still, talk of the incident persisted well into the 1950s. It even provided the plot for an episode of the 1950s television show *One Step Beyond*.

Those who believe it is nothing more than an urban legend think it started with a soldier seeing something strange. His account then morphed into a much more elaborate story over the decades.

But there are others who think that thousands of soldiers did see something strange in the sky on that evening.

One theory is that the mentally draining nature of warfare, especially trench warfare, induced a mass psychosis across Europe. Mass psychosis has been observed plenty of times throughout history, but this (if true) would be one of the biggest cases.

Then there are the more supernatural explanations.

Some believe it was a sign from god or angels to end the destruction before it was too late, while others think it was visitors from another planet. One thing is for sure, no matter the source of the light (if it even happened), there is little doubt that this story will continue to be told.

# Hatred for *Hogan's Heroes*

You've probably seen reruns of the hit American television show *Hogan's Heroes* and not really thought much about it. After all, it isn't a particularly deep show with any social relevancy, right? I mean, how could it be?

For those of you not familiar with *Hogan's Heroes*, it's a show about Allied prisoners of war in World War II who use their prison to coordinate top secret missions for the Allies and the anti-Nazi underground. The plots were far-fetched and the characters silly and purposefully campy, but the production values were high and it proved to be a major hit. The producers of the show successfully created a sitcom by buying into the spy craze of film and television of the late 1960s. It was good harmless fun, right?

Not everyone was happy with a sitcom based on the deadliest war in human history.

You might find this hard to believe, but the American Nazi Party protested the show for portraying the Nazis as bumbling fools. More believable were protests by Jewish groups who argued that *Hogan's Heroes* trivialized World War II. Despite the protests, or possibly because of it, the producers of *Hogan's Heroes* continued to do well in the ratings.

The reality is that the Nazis were actually more accurate in their criticism. Most of the major Nazi characters in the show were played by Jews, some of whom had been interred in concentration camps before the war, and all knew the risks that such a show could bring. In fact, Werner Klemperer, who played the eternally bumbling Colonel Klink, and was Jewish, once said in an interview: "I had one qualification when I took the job: if they ever wrote a segment whereby Colonel Klink would come out the hero, I would leave the show."

Much of the controversy about the show died down after knowledge of the cast's Nazi characters' ethnicity became known. By the late 1970s, after *Hogan's Heroes* had been off the air for several years, controversy surrounding the show surfaced again when Robert Crane, who played Colonel Hogan, was found murdered in a motel room.

We'll get to that story later.

# The Haunted Town

If you're ever passing through Kansas City and are up for a potentially frightening detour, you might be interested in driving just seven miles of Lawrence, Kansas to the tiny town of Stull, Kansas. The area around Stull was settled by German immigrants and, in the mid-1800s, the people built a church and cemetery, making those the centerpiece of what would become the unincorporated town of Stull.

Despite its potential, Stull never grew beyond fifty people and is all but abandoned today. Some say the town was just a victim of the times—as Americans flocked to suburbia after World War II, towns like Stull had nothing to offer.

But there are those who believe something more sinister was behind Stull's demise.

A couple of tragic deaths in Stull left a major impression in the minds of people in that area. First, there was a boy who was burned to death when his father set a fire to his land to clear away some brush. The other involved the mysterious death of a young man who had gone missing. He was found a few days later hanging from a tree: some say he committed suicide, while others believe he was murdered.

Then there was the town church and cemetery, which people began calling "one of the seven gateways into Hell" in the 1970s.

The origins of the legend are unclear. The first documented mention of the haunted church and cemetery appeared in a 1974 issue of the University of Kansas' student newspaper, *The University Daily Kansan*. Some of the details of the legend were outlined in that article. For example, on both Halloween and the Spring Equinox, a set of otherwise hidden steps appears near the church that leads to the deepest bowels of Hell!

There is no evidence that such a legend existed before the article was published, which would make sense because the church had already been closed for some time. And there had yet to be any tales of supernatural occurrences associated with the church or cemetery.

But 1974 was just on the heels of the counterculture movement, which included a plethora of New Age religious groups and more than a few cults.

By the early 1970s, self-appointed psychics, ghost hunters, and self-proclaimed Satanists began visiting the town on a regular basis. This led to the *Daily Kansan* article, which consequently popularized the story. By the late 1970s, Stull had become a popular destination for local high school and college kids looking for a little excitement. The cemetery became littered with beer cans, some of the tombstones were vandalized, and the church was regularly used as a party pad.

As all of this was happening, strange events continued: chilling sounds were heard, scary apparitions were seen, and many reported having car problems near the church and cemetery.

It all became too much for the Douglas County officials, who had the church demolished in 2002 and now regularly patrol the cemetery, especially on Halloween and the Spring Equinox.

Despite all of the strange occurrences associated with Stull, there are no confirmed reports that anyone ever took the steps into Hell. At least if someone did (and they survived the journey), they never said anything about it.

# The State of Superior

The size of the United States is generally seen as one of its strengths—it contains enough natural resources to sustain its residents and also to help feed other parts of the world. But the country's large size can also lead to some problems. The American Civil War was, at least partially, the result of two sections of the country growing in different directions: physically, culturally, and politically. Although there haven't been any violent secessionist movements since the mid-1800s, regional differences have led to some people trying to form new states and some even wanting complete independence for their state.

Superior is the name of the proposed state that would encompass the Upper Peninsula of Michigan, part of the Lower Peninsula, some counties in northern Wisconsin, and possibly some counties in northeastern Minnesota. The advocates of Superior argue that the counties in this region have more in common with each other—culturally and geographically— than they do with the states they currently belong to. Though the movement to create the state of Superior seems to have peaked in the 1970s, there are still advocates for it.

As strange as making a new state of Superior may sound, there are certainly precedents for it—Maine was once part of Massachusetts and Vermont was part of New York.

Another similar movement is the independence movement known as "Cascadia." Most Cascadian advocates want all or part of Washington, Oregon, northern California, Idaho, and part of the Canadian province of British Columbia to form a new nation-state. Some Cascadian plans also involve parts of the states of Montana and part of Alberta. The Cascadian movement is a little different than the Superior one though, as Cascadians advocate for a totally new and independent country.

Similar initiatives have been put forward in California, Alaska, Hawaii, and Texas.

It is impossible to say for sure if any of these statehood and independence movements will become a reality. But I think most people will agree that it is equally difficult to state without a doubt that the current borders of the United States will remain the same permanently.

# A Hunka Hunka Burning Love

On February 20, 1725, one of the strangest criminal cases in history happened in Rheims, France. On the morning in question, Jean Millet awakened in the inn he owned and operated with his wife. Surveying the establishment, he found a pile of ashes and a few internal organs in the kitchen. It turned out these were the remains of Jean's wife, Nicole.

During a time when modern science was in its relative infancy, the scene was particularly perplexing to investigators. There was little left of Nicole, which would indicate an extremely hot fire, but little else in the kitchen had been burned. The bizarre situation began to look especially bad for Jean when it was rumored that he was cheating on his alcoholic wife with one of the maids at the inn.

Jean was charged with murder and later convicted and sent to prison.

But Jean appealed his case, and during his second trial he called a young surgeon named Nicholas Le Cat to testify on his behalf. Le Cat argued on the stand that there was no way a person could have started a fire that would have consumed the body so quickly and without causing major damage to the rest of the room.

Mrs. Millet, therefore, must have been the victim of spontaneous combustion.

That's right, Jean Millet used the spontaneous combustion defense and actually won! In the centuries that have followed, this defense has never again been used at a murder trial. But there have been hundreds of other cases of spontaneous combustion throughout the world. These cases are rarely witnessed and usually involve someone finding a person's remains in a pile of ashes with little fire damage done to the surrounding area. As creepy and supernatural as spontaneous combustion may sound, scientists think that there is a logical explanation for most cases—the "wick effect."

This phenomenon takes place when the clothing of a burn victim soaks up the heated fat and acts like a wick, leading to an almost complete incineration of the body. Investigators have shown that in many of these cases the victims were smokers who fell asleep with a lit cigarette, which is what Le Cat believed happened in Nicole Millet's case. This surely sounds logical, but not every case of spontaneous combustion has involved smokers. So that leaves us with many unsolved cases of spontaneous combustion.

Luckily, cases of spontaneous combustion are so rare you probably don't have anything to worry about—unless you are a smoker, in which case this is just another good reason to quit.

# The "Big One"
# Hits the Midwest

No doubt you've heard about the giant earthquake known as the "Big One" that is supposed to hit California at some point in the future. Geologists are convinced that someday the San Andreas Fault, which runs through the middle of most of California, will someday move so much that it will cause a massive earthquake that could send much of Los Angeles, or San Francisco, or both, into the ocean. Since the 1970s, there have been numerous big budget films made about this scenario, but as of today, all of these movies remain science fiction.

Thankfully!

But if you think that the San Andreas Fault zone presents the only major serious earthquake threat to the United States, you're wrong. Located in the southeastern Missouri bootheel is a small town named New Madrid. The town itself is quaint and unassuming, an architectural and cultural blend of the Midwest and Southeast. But what lies beneath the ground could potentially kill millions.

Second only to the San Andreas Fault in size, the New Madrid Seismic Zone runs through the boot-heel north into the southern tip of Illinois and south into northeastern Arkansas for about 150 miles, which includes parts of the states of

Missouri, Kentucky, Illinois, and Tennessee. In modern times, the rumblings of the New Madrid zone haven't been nearly as remarkable compared to what has taken place in California, but it has quite a destructive history.

In December of 1811 and January of 1812, the New Madrid Fault Line erupted in a series of powerful earthquakes that changed the course of the Mississippi River. Although there were no instruments to gauge the strength of the earthquakes, geologists believe that the first quake measured 8.0 "moment magnitude," which would put it into the "Big One" category.

The quakes were felt hundreds of miles away and created the large northwest Tennessee lake, Reelfoot Lake.

The quakes even had a major impact on the history of the early American republic.

Many of the American Indian tribes of the region (now recognized as the states of Illinois and Indiana) took the quakes as a sign that they should align with the British against the Americans in the War of 1812. If you don't know how that one turned out, the Americans won. So maybe it was actually a sign for them to stay *out* of the war.

Fortunately, since that part of America was still the frontier, the quakes caused relatively few deaths. But that wouldn't be the case today.

Seismologists and geologists are conflicted over whether or not a "Big One" will happen in the New Madrid zone. However, all agree that if one were to happen it would be devastating for the region. Since the New Madrid zone is under the Mississippi River, it would cause major flooding, disrupt barge traffic, and destroy the handful of bridges between St. Louis and Memphis. The quake would also damage those two cities, potentially causing immense destruction and loss of life in Memphis.

So if you're living in the New Madrid zone or planning to move there, just take a cue from lifelong Californians — always be ready for an earthquake, but don't live in fear of the "Big One."

# Take My Hand, Really

We've all been in a situation where we are in a room and just want to leave. Usually it's because of the crowd: we don't feel comfortable around the other people in our company and just want to escape the area. It's a common situation, but one that doesn't happen often enough for it to seriously affect our lives.

But can you imagine what it would be like to feel as if part of your own body just didn't belong and was out of place?

Yes, a very miniscule percentage of people around the world, mainly men, feel that certain limbs on their bodies simply don't belong. Medical professionals have termed this affliction Body Integrity Dysphoria (BID) and there are only about three hundred known cases in history. BID creates major problems for those with the disorder.

Since BID has only been identified in recent years, much remains unknown about the disorder, including its origins and even possible methods of treatment. Interestingly, those afflicted with BID tend to fixate on the left side of their body, usually on their leg, although there are plenty of cases where the arm or hand represent the area of concern. There is a consensus in the mental health field that BID is a disorder, with some professionals believing it is sexual in nature.

Those afflicted with BID tend to let it control their lives. Oftentimes, they create contraptions that make them look as though they are an amputee, which can lead to social, personal, and economic problems.

Then there are the extreme cases.

There was the case of a mild-mannered man from the American Midwest named Jason who, from a young age, felt that his right hand just didn't belong. John was afflicted by negative feelings for years, but he never told anyone.

So he decided to take matters into his own hands, or hand!

One night he went into his garage, turned on his table saw, and sawed off his hand in one quick cut.

Although Jason lived to tell his story, there are others who have not, including an American who died from infection after having a limb amputated by a shady doctor in Tijuana, Mexico. It is unknown how many people suffering from BID have had limbs removed, but it has been reported that those who have, such as Jason, have reported significant improvements in their symptoms afterwards.

Still, medical professionals advise strongly against amputation if you suffer from this rare disease.

# The Smiley Face Murders

If you're a male college student in the Midwest, be careful the next time you're out drinking or you might end up the victim of the Smiley Face Killer. According to retired New York City Police detectives, Kevin Gannon and Anthony Duarte, and St. Cloud State University criminology professor Lee Gilberston, a person (or persons) has been targeting males—primarily white—who've had a bit too much to drink on or near college campuses in the Midwest. They believe that as many as forty-five young men have been killed by the Smiley Face Killer, so named because of the smiley-face graffiti found near some of the bodies.

Most of the men were found in rivers or lakes, with the local police believing they were drowning victims.

But Gannon, Duarte, and Gilbertson believe most of the men were forcibly drowned.

One potential victim was Dakota James, who called a friend on the evening of December 16, 2016 to pick him up from a motel. James told his friend that he was drinking with some other friends at bars in downtown Pittsburgh, Pennsylvania when he blacked out and came to in the motel. Five weeks later he vanished again, this time for good; his body was discovered weeks later, floating ten miles away in the Ohio River.

There were several smiley faces spray-painted on a nearby bridge.

Although the local police ruled James' death an accidental drowning, the date-rape drug GHB was found in his system, and the decomposition rate of his body showed he'd been in the water for a couple days at the most, not the forty days he had been missing. And after famed forensic analyst Cyril Wecht examined the autopsy photos, he determined that there were ligature marks on James' neck.

But Dakota James is one of only forty-five to one hundred young men whom Gannon, Duarte, and Gilberston believe were murdered by the Smiley Face Killer. From Fargo, North Dakota to Lacrosse, Wisconsin and from Massachusetts to Minnesota, numerous young, healthy, white men have been found floating in bodies of water with GHB in their systems and smiley faces nearby. Besides looking similar, many of these young men excelled in athletics and were studying STEM or medicine in college.

The investigative trio believes that the culprit is actually a well-organized gang or cult driven by hatred for the victims' demographic. They also believe there is a sexual-ritualistic aspect to the crimes.

But as creepy as these crimes are, not everyone believes they are the work of an organized conspiracy, or that they are even connected. The FBI has publicly stated that they have reviewed many of these cases and that they see no connections.

The FBI's denials have only added steam to some of the conspiracy theories floating around.

The work of these three investigators was enough for the American cable television network Oxygen to turn the case into a six-part 2019 series, *Smiley Face Killers: The Hunt for Justice.*

The majority of law enforcement remains unconvinced that there is a Smiley Face Killer on the loose. But if you're a young man who fits this particular demographic and are drinking in bars in the Midwest, you'd best watch your drink and stay on guard.

# The City That Wouldn't Die

Since man first began building and living in urban settlements about five thousand years ago, countless cities have come and gone. Many early cities couldn't keep pace with others that were better equipped for success due to their locations near resources, while some were the victims of warfare. Cities that were destroyed by warfare were occasionally rebuilt once or twice, but rarely more than that.

But if you go just outside of the modern Turkish town of Hisarlik, you'll find a large mound that is the final resting place of a city that had nine lives. In ancient times, it was known as Troy. Yes, the legendary Troy that was sieged for ten years by the Greeks. It was discovered and excavated by German archaeologist Heinrich Schliemann in 1870s, proving that the Troy of the *Odyssey, Iliad,* and *Aeneid* really was true, to a certain extent. When news of Schliemann's discovery spread around the world, many were overjoyed to learn that the seemingly useless classes in Greek history they were forced to take were actually somewhat validated.

But those in academic circles were even more excited.

Schliemann's excavations illuminated facts about Mycenaean Greece and Hittite Anatolia that were previously only theories, such as the extent of Mycenaean influence in the Aegean. The excavations also helped scholars fill in chronological gaps in the Late Bronze Age, which were at least partially the result of the so-called Sea Peoples invasions around 1200 BC. And as more and more excavations took place at the site in the decades and after Schliemann's initial discovery, it was learned that the city, also known as Ilion, had begun as early as 3000 BC, when man first began building urban settlements.

Troy was destroyed through warfare and abandoned time after time. Then it was rebuilt by people possibly related to the Hittite Civilization around 1300 BC, which is today known as Troy VIIa. This was the Troy of the Homeric epics.

Even after the Mycenaean Greeks destroyed Troy VIIa, the settlement was rebuilt again and became a favored city of the Romans. Unlike the Greeks, who knew they were descended from the besiegers of Troy, the Romans believed they were descendants of the Trojans. During the reign of Emperor Augustus in the first century BC-AD, Troy was given the Latin name Ilium and continued to have favored status. The Romans installed baths and built an amphitheater in the city, but as Roman power faded so too did Troy's allure. When the Western Roman Empire collapsed in AD 476, Troy IX, the final Troy, also came to an end.

As Christians, the Byzantine Greeks were much less interested in Troy and simply ignored the site. When the Ottoman Turks—who also had no interest in pagan myths—conquered the region, they built a new settlement, Hisarlik, near the forgotten city.

But thanks to the efforts of Heinrich Schliemann, Troy was once more given new life, confirming its reputation as a city that will not die.

# Exploding Trees

Most of you reading this have probably experienced a lightning storm at some point in your life. As the clouds above crash, creating thunder, and the static and charged particles in the air create the lightning that goes with it, most of us are smart enough to find cover, which is why lightning storms claim very few lives every year.

But they do kill thousands of trees per year.

You've probably toured an area after a particularly strong lightning storm, awestricken to find the horribly mangled remains of trees that were more than a hundred years old. You also probably remember being told as a kid to stay away from trees during a lightning storm. But have you ever considered the science behind the warning?

Of course, it seems logical that a tree would act as a lightning rod, especially if it is the tallest thing in the middle of a field. But trees are made of wood, and wood is supposed to be an insulator, not a conductor of electricity. So why do so many get hit with lightning? It happens for the same reason that they also explode.

Trees, like animals and people, are living organisms that need a fair amount of water to survive. The tallness of trees may be what makes them susceptible to lightning strikes, but it is the water the lightning is attracted to and what makes the strikes so fatal.

As soon as lightning hits a tree, it turns the tree's water into gas, causing its outer layers to explode, which is where trees store most of their water. About 50 percent of trees hit by a bolt of lightning die immediately after, and a small percentage more die in the ensuing months, usually during the winter. If one of your trees is hit by lightning and survives the initial assault, you should give it plenty of water and fertilizer. It may also help to cut away branches that will probably die anyway.

# When Reality Imitates Art

Many people consider Stephen King to be the modern master of horror, and for good reason. He has written hundreds of novels, novellas, and short stories that have frightened millions of people. Dozens of his stories have been turned into films, such as the 1984 novel *Thinner*, which was later turned into a 1996 film of the same name.

If you aren't familiar with *Thinner*, it is the story of an obese and greedy but well-connected lawyer who is cursed by a Gypsy. The main character's trouble begins when his wife gives him a blowjob while he's driving. Distracted behind the wheel, he hits and kills an elderly Gypsy. The main character uses his connections to beat the manslaughter charge, but is subsequently cursed by a Gypsy who touches his face and whispers "thinner." The obese man quickly starts to lose weight. By the end of the story, he has all but withered away.

As interesting as the plot of *Thinner* may sound, what happened to Stephen King on June 19, 1999 is even more interesting.

Around 4:30 p.m. that evening, King was walking along the shoulder of the state highway near his home in Maine, as he had done countless times in the past. A man named Bryan Smith, who was distracted by a dog in his van, was driving along the same route.

Smith hit King and sent him flying about fourteen feet. King was rushed to the hospital where he stayed for nearly a month and had to undergo five operations. He had a collapsed lung and one of his legs was so badly shattered that the doctors considered amputating it. King's status was touch-and-go for a couple of weeks. Even after he was released from the hospital, it was a long road to recovery for the horror and sci-fi writer.

Smith was charged with the felony of aggravated assault due to his negligence. But, just like in *Thinner*, he later pleaded guilty to a lesser charge and was given a suspended jail sentence.

Then things got really strange.

Smith was found dead from an apparent fentanyl overdose on September 21, 2000. The death was ruled a suicide by the authorities, but the date is important because it happened to be Stephen King's birthday! When asked about the death, King said in an interview, "I was very sorry to hear of the passing of Bryan Smith. The death of a 43-year-old man can only be termed untimely."

Untimely, or something from another world?

# Before Columbus

Earlier, we learned how most of us were given false information by our grade school teachers when they told us the leaders of Europe believed the earth was flat in the fifteenth century. Thanks to Ptolemy, Columbus knew the world was a sphere and that he wouldn't fall off as he sailed across the Atlantic to Asia, or the Americas. But our teachers were right when they told us Columbus was the first outsider to discover America, right?

Well, not really.

Of course, the Americas were populated by numerous indigenous tribes and peoples, some of them quite sophisticated, such as the Mayans, Incas, and Aztecs. But those people were, for the most part, native to the land and therefore didn't "discover" it. For centuries, Christopher Columbus was believed to have been the first nonindigenous person to discover the Americas, but in the 1960s that idea began to be challenged by different theories.

Let's start with some of the stranger theories.

One theory that has come up from time to time is that the ancient Phoenicians landed on the east coast sometime in the first millennium BC. The Phoenicians were known for their seafaring prowess, but their activities were primarily limited to the Mediterranean Sea. Those who believe the Phoenicians discovered America think that one or more of their ships were blown off course and ended up in the northeast United States. As proof, advocates point to some potential pieces of evidence, such as the "Dighton Rock" in Massachusetts. The Dighton Rock is a rock originally discovered in the seventeenth century that has what appears to be undeciphered writing on it.

Other theories have placed the Romans, Greeks, and even the Hebrews in the Americas based on little to no evidence.

One of the most interesting theories of Old World contact with the Americas came from Norwegian explorer Thor Heyerdahl. Heyerdahl believed that the ancient Egyptians could have made the trip across the Atlantic Ocean on boats made of papyrus. Based on ancient Egyptian depictions of their boats, Heyerdahl constructed a boat he named the "Ra." In 1969, he left Morocco with a small crew for the Americas. The Ra failed, but one year later, he and his crew left Morocco again in the "Ra II" and made it to the Caribbean.

Heyerdahl's voyage fascinated the world and proved that such a trip *could have* been done. But scholars were quick to point out that it didn't prove the trip was ever made.

Still another theory is that Chinese explorer Zheng He discovered the west coast of what would become America in the early fifteenth century, about fifty years before Columbus landed in the Caribbean. As with the other alternative theories, there is no documentation that proves this theory, and nearly every mainstream Chinese historian has stated that it is a "pseudo history."

So that leaves us with the Vikings.

More than five hundred years before Columbus sailed across the Atlantic, the Vikings were making their own incredible journeys: They discovered and colonized many islands in the North Atlantic on their way to colonizing Greenland in the late tenth and early eleventh centuries. The Vikings' presence in Greenland is well-documented through archaeological evidence and "sagas" that were written by Icelandic poets in later decades and centuries. Among the sagas written about Greenland were ones that described "Vinland." To many scholars, Vinland sounded a lot like North America: It was home to "Skraelings" who sounded very much like American Indians, and the flora and fauna also matched that of North America.

Historians and archaeologists searched and searched for evidence of Vinland in America, sometimes coming up with false leads. Finally, in the 1960s, the remains of a small Viking Age settlement were discovered near L'Anse Aux Meadows, Labrador, Canada. The structure and style of the homes found at the site, in addition to unearthed iron artifacts, proved that Vikings did in fact settle in North America.

And they did so nearly five hundred years before Columbus made his voyage.

# The World's Deepest Hole

Do you remember when you were a kid, out playing with your friends, and someone decided to try to dig a hole to China? After digging for a while, you probably got bored, decided to do something else, and forgot all about the endeavor. If you did happen to remember it, you probably realized at some point that it is impossible to dig a hole to China. And even if you could dig a hole through the earth, chances are you wouldn't end up in China.

So, you moved on to more important things in your life. But have you ever wondered about the biggest hole on the planet?

It happens to be the Mariana Trench. The Mariana Trench is a fifteen hundred-mile-long, forty-mile-wide trench in the Pacific Ocean, about one hundred twenty miles east of the Mariana Islands. The deepest parts of the trench are believed to be more than thirty-five thousand feet deep, but since it is so deep, getting accurate readings have been difficult. The Mariana Trench was formed by two tectonic plates colliding against each other, which also happened to form the Mariana Islands. Because there is very little life that far beneath the ocean, and the available technology makes a journey that deep expensive and difficult, few trips have been made.

Interestingly, film director James Cameron, who is best known for *Titanic*, made the descent to the bottom of the Mariana Trench in 2012. His was only the second manned dive to reach the bottom, making it to a depth of over thirty-five thousand feet.

So, the next time you see some kids planning to dig a hole to China, tell them to start in the Mariana Trench.

# Disappearing Witnesses

Mark Dutroux is probably the most hated man in Belgium. He is the small European country's most notorious serial killer, having murdered at least eleven people during the 1990s. It isn't the number of victims that makes Dutroux so hated, but the age of his victims and some of the details of his case. Many of his victims were preteen girls who he, along with his wife Michelle Martin, abducted, raped, and murdered. After torturing his victims for weeks on end, sometimes in one of his many homes, he would often bury them alive in his backyard.

The worst part is that the Belgian authorities had known about Dutroux since at least 1986.

In 1986, Dutroux was a thirty-year-old-man with plenty of money and properties, but no real legitimate income. He stole cars for a living, and when he wasn't stealing cars, he was abducting and raping girls with Martin, who was his girlfriend at the time. The police eventually caught up with the pair and convicted Dutroux of five abduction-rapes, but Dutroux was only given a thirteen-year sentence and was released after serving just three years.

Many people believe that that was the first sign that Dutroux had deep connections in Belgian society.

When Dutroux was captured in 1996, his reign of terror finally came to an end. But a new—and even more bizarre—chapter in his case began. The police bungled evidence from Dutroux's home, and it was revealed that they had known something about his activities since at least 1995. Then the case seemed to drag on for years.

And then one of Dutroux's accomplices, Michael Lelievre, publicly claimed that they were part of a highly organized pedophilia and sex trafficking conspiracy.

Lelievre pointed the finger at a Brussels businessman named Jean Michel Nihoul, claiming he was one of the major facilitators of the conspiracy. In October of 1996, after all of this came to the surface, nearly three hundred thousand Belgians marched on the capital seeking answers.

They received few.

Although Dutroux and Martin received life sentences and will more than likely never be released from prison, reports about the conspiracy continue to surface. Women who claim to be survivors state that Dutroux was just a hired grunt who procured girls and drugs for well-connected politicians, businessmen, professors, judges, and even members of law enforcement. With that said, many in Belgium's law enforcement community worked to uncover any potential conspiracy but were seemingly thwarted at every step.

The original judge of Dutroux's case, Jean-Marc Connerotte, was fired for no apparent reason by a judge well past his prime who seemed more interested in collecting a paycheck than in finding the truth. But even more chilling were the deaths of all the witnesses connected to the case.

There were twenty unexplained deaths of witnesses involved with Dutroux's case—some were inexplicable murders while others were labeled "accidents." These deaths certainly add fuel to the conspiracy theories still circulating about the case.

It seems unlikely that Dutroux will ever tell the complete story about the murders. Well, maybe on his deathbed.

# Not Your Average Aliens

Nearly half of the American population believes in the existence of intelligent alien life-forms, and about 20 percent of Americans believe they've seen a UFO at some point in their lives. Of course, what constitutes a UFO sighting varies widely. Upon close inspection, most are determined to have origins that are quite terrestrial in nature.

Then there is the tiny percentage of people who've actually claimed to have seen aliens and made some sort of contact with them—a "Close Encounter of the Third Kind."

After the Roswell UFO incident in 1947, the term UFO became a normal part of the American—and then the world's—vocabulary. It also seemed as though sightings began to increase progressively in the following decades. UFO sightings turned into somewhat of a craze until they peaked in the 1990s—numerous documentaries were made such as the now-debunked *Alien Autopsy*. The UFO craze also influenced the fiction of the 1990s, which is when the popular television show *The X Files* began its long run and the *Men in Black* series first started.

In nearly all of these documentaries, television episodes, and movies, aliens are usually depicted as short with gray skin, long fingers, and large, bulbous heads featuring slits where the nose, eyes, and mouth are located on humans. But not all Close Encounters of the Third Kind have been with these

"Grays." Several reported encounters occurred with aliens who looked more like Arnold Schwarzenegger in his prime.

This class of aliens has been termed "Nordic Aliens."

People who claim to have made contact with this special class of extraterrestrials describe them as six to seven feet tall, blonde-haired with fair complexions, and blue eyes. Most of the Nordic Aliens reported have been males, although occasionally they have been accompanied by females. Nearly every encounter with these aliens has been positive: They often communicate telepathically and express a desire to help humans overcome social and political problems.

Sightings of the Nordic Aliens began shortly after Roswell Incident, but decreased in the 1970s. Although there are still occasional claimed sightings of these beings, they lag far behind the Grays and are virtually unknown to many young people. True believers think that the Nordic Aliens have either given their message and have moved on, are living among us as Earthlings, or have left but are waiting to return when the planet reaches a point of critical mass.

Of course, not everyone is convinced Nordic Aliens exist.

Some experts claim that Nordic Aliens are just a projection of peoples' hopes and fears and that the height of their sightings coincided, by no coincidence, with the Civil Rights Movement in America.

Still, those who claim to have made contact with the Nordic Aliens remain convinced they exist and that they will one day return to show humanity the way forward.

# I'm Billy the Kid

You probably know a little about the notorious Wild West outlaw known as Billy the Kid, who was born Henry McCarty in 1859 but often went by the alias William Bonney. You may have studied him in a history class and/or became introduced to his exploits in the *Young Guns* movies from the 1980s.

If you aren't familiar with Billy the Kid, here is a brief rundown.

Billy came to fame during the 1880s, when he was a major player in a range war in New Mexico Territory. After killing at least three men, he was captured and put in jail, then killed two deputies during an escape. According to historical record, Billy went on the lam for a couple of months. He was then shot and killed by Sheriff Pat Garrett in Fort Sumner, New Mexico, which is where his grave is located. . . supposedly.

Not long after the reported shooting of Billy the Kid, conspiracy theories began to circulate that his death was an elaborate hoax. The theory, which is not improbable, states that Garrett and Billy staged the death, as the two men were actually friends. Afterwards, they split the reward money and Billy left the area to live out his life under a different identity.

The reality is that, in 1881, it wouldn't have been too difficult to create such a hoax. As a sheriff, Garrett had the authority to sign off on any death certificate, and he had the power to keep inquisitive people away from the body. It is curious that there are no known photographs of Billy the Kid's body, which is a bit strange considering that it was common to photograph the corpses of known criminals at the time.

One of the first men who was suspected to be Billy the Kid was an Arizonan named John Miller. The first public record of Miller is an August 8, 1881 marriage certificate, which was just three weeks after Billy was killed by Garrett. He married a Mexican woman and moved to Arizona where he became a successful rancher. Interestingly, Miller never claimed to be Billy the Kid; some of his family members came forward in the 1930s with the claim.

Miller was said to have had permanent injuries from a gunshot wound, and he definitely had some physical similarities to Billy the Kid.

But the claimant to Billy the Kid's identity who received the most attention was Brushy Bill Roberts.

Roberts was a wily old Texas ranch hand who was fond of tall tales when he entered the scene in 1948. During that year, a Texas lawyer located an elderly man who claimed to be a veteran of the Lincoln County, New Mexico Range War and who asserted that Billy the Kid was still alive and living in Texas.

Brushy Bill was located and, sure enough, he claimed to be Billy the Kid. He even requested a pardon from the governor of New Mexico for his crimes, but he was denied. Brushy Bill died in 1951 and was quickly forgotten about until he was used as a character in the *Young Guns* movies. The movies led to more interest and the case was then profiled on an episode of *Unsolved Mysteries*. Due to the limits of science at the time, however, there was little that anyone could do to prove or disprove the story.

Finally, as DNA testing became more common and affordable in the 2000s, a DNA sample was taken from Miller's exhumed body. It was then compared to blood drops taken from the wooden floor of the Lincoln County jail that were believed to have come from Billy the Kid. Unfortunately, the sample from the jail was too degraded to make a match.

Investigators next planned to exhume Billy's mother and Brushy Bill, but neither have been exhumed as of the writing of this book.

Perhaps this will be one mystery that will forever remain unsolved—a fascinating chapter belonging to the legend and lore of America's frontier history.

# Lingua Franca

You've probably heard the term *lingua franca* at some point in your life. *Lingua franca* is simply a "common language" used to facilitate trade, diplomacy, or other functions where people of different backgrounds come together for a common purpose.

The origin of the term can be traced to the Mediterranean region during the Middle Ages, where merchants and sailors used a sort of pidgin/hybrid language to communicate with each other. The Latin term *lingua franca* began to be used at that time to describe this new hybrid language—lingua means "language" and franca means "Frank," so translated literally it means "language of the Franks"—which was heavily influenced by French.

Not long after the Mediterranean pidgin fell out of use in the 1700s, French did in fact become the *lingua franca* of the Western world. Most of the world's leaders and merchants knew at least some French, and most of America's founding fathers were fluent in the language of love.

But *lingua franca* languages predate the term by several centuries.

The ancient Semitic language Akkadian was probably the first *lingua franca* of the world. Akkadian was the native language of Babylon, but by the Late Bronze Age (ca. 1500-1200 BC) it was used by the nobles and merchants of the Egyptian, Hittite, Assyrian, and Babylonian empires as a common language. After Akkadian fell out of use in late antiquity, Aramaic took its place in the Near East. You might be surprised to know that Aramaic, not Hebrew, was Jesus' first language!

After the Romans conquered the Mediterranean basin and ventured north into Europe and east to Mesopotamia, Latin became the *lingua franca* of their vast empire.

Today, English has become the *lingua franca* of the world, but just like our other examples, it too will fall out of favor at some point.

Perhaps we should prepare for the next *lingua franca* by learning Mandarin.

# Get Outta Dodge!

If you're an American, you've either used the phrase "Get Outta Dodge" or heard the phrase spoken at some point in your life. Chances are, you probably also know the origin of the term. If you don't, that is a story worth telling. The phrase refers to the city of Dodge City, Kansas, which was a popular stomping ground for cowboys moving stock north from Texas in the late 1800s. Several famous people from the Old West went through Dodge, including legendary lawman Wyatt Earp.

But as interesting as all that may be, the phrase "Get Outta Dodge" didn't become common until after America's longest-running live-action television show, *Gunsmoke*, hit the air in 1955. When the show was finally cancelled twenty years later, six hundred thirty-five episodes had been produced. Not only were most Americans familiar with Marshal Matt Dillon, Miss Kitty, Doc, and Festus, but audiences around the world came to love this quintessentially American epic.

*Gunsmoke* actually began as a radio show in 1952, but the popularity of the Western genre in general, and the show in particular, led TV producers to transition it to the small screen. It didn't take long for the show to build a large fan base and do well in the ratings.

Unlike other Westerns of the time, *Gunsmoke* often took a grittier and harsher view of life on the frontier.

For example, Marshal Dillon didn't always get his man and sometimes the innocent were hanged. Marshall Dillon's primary love interest, Miss Kitty, was a saloon/brothel owner and was herself a former "saloon girl." Despite its sometimes dark tone, *Gunsmoke* rarely moralized, unlike some other Westerns of the period, such as *Bonanza* and *Big Valley*.

Over the course of its long run, *Gunsmoke* saw many regular actors come and also featured a number of guest stars on single episodes. Many famous actors got their start on *Gunsmoke* in somewhat surprising roles. For instance, Lenard Nimoy, best known as Spock in the *Star Trek* franchise, played an Indian on an early episode.

There were also some cases where actors played guest stars in different roles in several episodes. Ken Curtis, who played Marshal Dillon's most memorable sidekick, Festus Hagen, appeared in one episode as a con artist ladies' man named Kyle and in another episode as an Indian scout.

And of course, *Gunsmoke* is where Burt Reynolds got his start when he played "half-breed" Quint Asper from 1962 to 1965.

Amazingly, James Arness, who played Matt Dillon, appeared in every episode of the show. And it wasn't until 2018 that the *Simpsons*, an animated show, beat *Gunsmoke* for the record of most scripted American-made television shows.

# Murder on the Greyhound Express

Those of us who have ridden the Greyhound Line in North America know that it can get pretty sketchy sometimes. Fights, drug deals and usage, and prostitution are all known to have taken place there, and that's just in the terminals! As twenty-two-year-old Canadian man Tim McLean unfortunately found out, things can get much worse on the buses.

On July 30, 2008, McLean was taking a Greyhound bus home to Winnipeg, Manitoba, Canada from a carnival job in Edmonton Alberta. It was a long ride that was almost coming to an end that evening—the bus was less than fifty miles from its destination.

At one of the last stops before Winnipeg, a Chinese-born Canadian citizen named Vincent Weiguang Li got on the bus. Li was not a particularly impressive individual to say the least. He had worked as a software engineer in his native China, but after he immigrated to Canada in 2001, he never really seemed to find solid footing. He attended a church in Winnipeg for a while, worked some menial jobs in the area, and then moved to Edmonton with his wife to work more menial jobs before getting fired from a Wal-Mart store.

To the few people who knew Li, things were quickly spiraling out of control for him.

When Li got on the bus that night he initially sat near the front of the bus. Then he slowly made his way to the back of the bus and took an open seat next to McLean.

McLean was sound asleep with his headphones on. . . . he never had a chance!

Suddenly, Li took out a large knife and began stabbing and hacking away at McLean. The bus driver did his best to protect the other passengers by ushering them out to the side of the road. He then tried to stop Li's homicidal fury, but it was too late. All the bus driver could do was call the local police.

And watch the disgusting display of depravity.

Li proceeded to chop McLean's head off, which he then pressed against the window to show the terrified passengers on the side of the road. He then began cutting pieces of flesh from his victim and ate them.

Local police and the Royal Canadian Mounted Police arrived on the scene at 9:00 p.m. and, after nearly a four-hour standoff, took Li into custody. Li was promptly charged with McLean's murder and faced the possibility of spending the rest of his life in a maximum security provincial prison in Manitoba. And it sure seemed like an airtight case.

What defense could he actually have for committing such a heinous crime?

Well, in the modern justice system in Western countries things don't always happen as expected.

Li pleaded "not criminally responsible," which in Canada is essentially a "not guilty by reason of insanity" plea. Instead of a jury deciding the merits of the plea, it was up to a judge. The judge ruled in Li's favor and sent him to a secure mental hospital in 2009. Now you might be thinking, "But they'll keep him in there for the rest of his life, right?" Well, not exactly.

Li's doctors stated that he responded well to treatment and, as a result, he was allowed unsupervised furloughs into the neighboring towns beginning in 2014. He was then released with no conditions in 2017, changed his name, and disappeared back into Canadian society.

If you're reading this in Canada, especially Manitoba, the Greyhound cannibal may be living next door to you and you'd never know it.

# Sequoyah, Where Did You Go?

Few American Indians were as impactful and important to their people and America as Sequoyah. Born in the late 1700s to a Cherokee mother and a German father in what is today eastern Tennessee, Sequoyah suffered a physical disability. This apparently pushed him in the direction of more academic pursuits.

He worked as a silversmith and, despite a debilitating limp, fought against other Indian tribes in more than one battle. But his true contribution to the world was made in the early 1800s. Sequoyah wanted to raise the living standard of the Cherokee people to that of the whites, and he knew that could only be accomplished through proper and formal education. But that would be difficult because most Cherokees at the time only spoke Cherokee and the Cherokee language had no written language.

So, Sequoyah created a syllabary/script for the Cherokee language.

Sequoyah's efforts immediately bore fruit as the new script was used to produce Cherokee-language newspapers and Cherokee literacy rates skyrocketed. He immediately became a leader among his people and was actually quite respected throughout America in general. But the government's policy of "Indian removal" meant that the Cherokees of the southeast would be uprooted and forced to move to Indian Territory (Oklahoma).

The Cherokees became a splintered nation. Most moved to Indian Territory/Oklahoma, but a small number were allowed to stay in western North Carolina and eastern Tennessee. Others decided to try their luck in the wild country of the borderland between Texas and Mexico.

In 1842, Sequoyah and a small group of his closest friends and family members set out to find the lost Cherokees in Mexico, which is where the mystery of his life begins, and ends.

Sequoyah and his band traveled among indigenous groups in northern Mexico and even taught some of them Cherokee, but they never found any of the lost Cherokee bands. Those in Sequoyah's group claimed that he died in August of 1843, but they gave few details and none concerning his manner of death.

The official record says that Sequoyah died in 1843 in the town of San Fernando (now Zaragoza), Tamaulipas, Mexico. There is no evidence to suggest that he died from violence and, since he was relatively old at the time, most scholars believe he died of natural causes. But within a few years of Sequoyah's supposed death, alternative theories began circulating.

Many believe that Sequoyah lived years past 1843 — some say 1845, while others place his death sometime in the 1850s. Questions over Sequoyah's death and possible resting place led the Cherokee Nation to fund an expedition to locate the leader's grave in 1939, but the findings were inconclusive. It was then revealed in 2011 that Sequoyah was buried in the Wichita Mountains of Oklahoma. According to this theory, two men discovered the skeletal remains of a man in a cave who had a crippled leg and was buried with a long-stemmed pipe.

The physical characteristics sound like Sequoyah, but the remains were never disinterred and their current location remains a mystery. There is also the question of why Sequoyah's remains would be in Oklahoma when he was traveling through northern Mexico when he died?

Well, the alternate theories hold that once Sequoyah realized that there were no lost bands of Cherokees living in the wilds of northern Mexico, he decided to go back home to Indian Territory/Oklahoma to live out his last days. Unfortunately, he died just before making it home and was buried in a cave.

As it now stands, it looks like the date of Sequoyah's death and his final resting place will forever remain one of history's mysteries.

# The Loch Ness Monster's American Cousins

Since the 1970s, the Loch Ness Monster has become so famous that it doesn't need much of an introduction. The craze surrounding the monster's existence, however, has faded quite a bit since the 1980s. Basically, for several decades, there have been sporadic sightings of a large aquatic creature in Loch Ness, Scotland. A few pictures have been captured, as well as a grainy film, but none of those have ever been proven to be authentic. Believers in the monster think it is actually a group of Jurassic Period aquatic dinosaurs (known as plesiosauruses) that somehow escaped extinction. All reported sightings of the Loch Ness monster describe a form and length (twenty to thirty feet) that sounds similar to the plesiosaurus.

Of course, academics are skeptical that a breeding population of plesiosauruses could have survived this long without being definitively discovered. You would think at least one of their bodies would've washed up on shore by now, right?

Minor details, like the lack of a body, haven't stopped interest, or sightings, of "Nessie" (as the Loch Ness Monster is often affectionately called), nor have they stopped similar sightings in the good ole U.S. of A.

That's right, America has a couple of its own versions of the Loch Ness Monster!

Located primarily in Vermont, but spilling over the international border into Quebec, Lake Champlain is believed by many locals to be the home of one or more creatures known as "Champ." Although there have been far fewer sightings of Champ than Nessie, most witnesses report seeing a similar a plesiosaurus type creature emerge from the lake before quickly going under water.

A 1977 photograph taken by local Sandra Messi certainly makes it seem like there could be some large creature swimming in the water, but skeptics believe the object in question is merely a floating log. Still, people continue to claim to see the creature to this day. In 2003, a team with the Discovery Channel even recorded sounds coming from the lake that were like those of small whales or dolphins.

Because it is an inland lake, Lake Champlain may seem like an unlikely place to house Nessie's American cousin, but a further look at the lake reveals that it is actually very similar to Loch Ness. Like the latter, it is very long, at over one hundred miles, but fairly narrow, with a maximum width of fourteen miles. With an average depth of sixty-four feet, t would also be deep enough to hide a few such creatures.

The locals of Lake Champlain certainly believe in Champ—or at least they say so for the sake of tourist dollars.

Another one of Nessie's American cousins inhabits the waters of the Chesapeake Bay and has become known as "Chessie." There are even fewer sightings of Chessie than Champ and photographic evidence is also less convincing. The descriptions of Chessie also differ slightly from that of Champ and Nessie, which suggests that he may belong to a different Jurassic family.

Chessie has been described as being about the same length as

Champ and Nessie, but more like a long zeuglodon than a plesiosaurus.

Since the Chesapeake Bay is connected directly to the Atlantic Ocean, Chessie's true identity presents a host of possibilities, including manta rays, sharks, small whales, or even escaped/released anaconda snakes.

One thing is for sure, if these creatures really do exist this would make for one interesting family reunion!

# The Sound of Heat

We've all been subjected to silly, inane conversations in our life, often over a few drinks and usually at a bar. These conversations usually involve one person who claims that something that is clearly fiction is actually a fact, and no matter what, you just can't convince them otherwise. The one example that comes to my mind is hearing someone declare that ten pounds of iron is heavier than ten pounds of cotton. No matter how many times you explain to your friend that a pound is the same weight no matter the substance, they just can't seem to get it through their stubborn head.

But occasionally you'll hear something that sounds really wrong, only to discover that it is actually true. This is the case with the sound of water. Yes, it's true. It turns out that hot and cold water actually make different sounds when they are being poured.

I didn't believe this myself when I first heard it from my friend at a bar several years ago, but it turns out he was right.

Hot water produces a higher-pitched sound when poured into a glass than cold water. The science behind this phenomenon relates to the viscosity of water. You've probably heard the term "viscosity" before in relation to the oil in your car, but it actually refers to the "thickness" of any liquid.

Yes, even water has a thickness.

Heat changes the viscosity of water, and all liquids for that matter, by energizing the molecules and making the liquid flow more, giving it a different sound when it splashes in a glass or cup. This is easier to see in other non-water liquids. Let's go back to oil, for instance. Motor oil is somewhat thick when it comes out the can, but when it's in your car being heated it's transformed into a more fluid substance, which produces a different sound.

This is the kind of scientific fact that can be proven just about anywhere, even at the bar.

# Strange Signals

If you're a shortwave radio enthusiast, or if you've had the chance to travel through Russia, then you may have heard one of three strangest radio stations ever known to man: UVB-76 (The Buzzer), 5448/3756 kHz (The Pip), and 3828/5473 (The Squeaky Wheel). Now, as much as these names might sound like normal nicknames that the stations adopted because they're easier to remember than their numbers, these are actually names given to them due to the sounds they broadcast. You see, these radio stations are named for the bizarre sounds that they emit—a buzzer, a beep, and a siren-type sound, respectively.

Little is known about these mysterious radio stations other than that they are based in Russia and are believed to move from time to time. UVB-76 is the best known of the three stations because it is believed to have been in operation since at least 1973, when the transmissions began getting picked up in the West. Shortwave radio listeners were amazed to hear the constant buzzers and beeps of the stations, even more so when these monotonous sounds were interrupted.

The Pip and The Squeaky Wheel sometimes broadcast what sounds like coded messages in Russian.

Listeners of The Buzzer have also picked up what sounded like phone conversations in Russian from possibly unaware technicians in the studio.

Most familiar with the radio stations believe that they are all connected, but it's anyone's guess as to what their purposes are. Although the Iron Curtain officially came down in 1991, the Russian government has not been forthcoming about these mysterious stations.

Most believe that the stations are somehow connected to the military, but their functions are anyone's guess. Some think that they served as an archaic form of communication during the Cold War and are now obsolete but were never shut down due to inefficiencies in the Russian bureaucracy. One of the more ominous explanations is that they are part of the Soviet Era "Dead Hand" system. The Dead Hand system was developed by the Soviet Union during the Cold War to counter America's first strike capabilities. Because the Americans had more sophisticated weapons and were capable of destroying much of the Soviet's communications infrastructure with a first strike, the Soviets developed a backup system that would give them the ability to call a second strike.

Although it has never been confirmed, it is widely believed that Russians have continued to employ the Dead Hand system after the collapse of the Soviet Union. Many believe that, due to their mysterious nature and the fact their physical locations have been moved, these three radio stations are part of the Dead Hand system.

If the signals stop, it could trigger the Russian nuclear arsenal.

Just to be on the safe side, let's hope these three stations keep broadcasting their weird signals.

# The Dangerous Game?

Amid the Satanic Panic of the 1980s, and clearly related to it, was sensationalism around the popular role-playing game *Dungeons & Dragons*, simply known as "D & D" by the players. Newspaper articles, "investigative journalists," and a host of religious figures warned America's mothers and fathers to watch their sons carefully and to make sure they weren't falling into the evil grasp of *Dungeons & Dragons*. To prove their point, they used a variety of examples of murder and mayhem. But a closer look reveals that, like much of the Satanic Panic, the *D & D* claims were overexaggerated.

*Dungeons & Dragons* was the brainchild of game designers Gary Gygax and Dave Arneson in the 1970s. It wasn't the first role-playing game to appear on the market, but after it was first published in 1974, it quickly became the most popular.

For the first few years of *Dungeons & Dragons'* existence, it went largely unnoticed by the media and religious leaders. Most of the people who knew anything about it thought it was a silly activity from the Counterculture Movement for boys with no girlfriends.

But as the culture of America changed in the 1980s, so too did its view of *Dungeons & Dragons*.

For those of you not familiar with the game, the players essentially pretend to be characters in a fantasy world that is heavily influenced by ancient and medieval history and mythology. Because of its subject matter, some religious leaders railed against the game as a gateway to Satanism, or worse—violent cult activity. Whether most of those religious leaders actually believed that *Dungeons & Dragons* was the spawn of Satan, or if they just grabbed on to the hysteria to elicit donations, is a matter of debate. But the mainstream media's role in the situation is not.

Normally, conservative Christian leaders and the mainstream media are not allies in America. But when it came to *D & D* in the 1980s, they both had a common message: the game was undoubtedly a bad influence on America's youth.

The popular news program *60 Minutes* aired a segment in 1985 that featured the game's creators on one side versus a woman named Patricia Pulling on the other. Pulling became an anti-*Dungeons & Dragons* activist after her son committed suicide in 1982.

She was convinced the game made him do it.

Then there was the 1988 murder of Leith von Stein and the attempted murder of his wife Bonnie. The police investigation of the brutal stabbing and bludgeoning attack quickly focused on Bonnie's son and Leith's stepson, Christopher Pritchard, and two of his friends. Christopher and his friends were convicted of murder, along with other charges, and given lengthy prison sentences for a crime that the prosecutors said was carried out purely for greed.

But it was also revealed that the three young men liked to drink booze, smoke pot, and play *Dungeons & Dragons* in the steam tunnels beneath North Carolina State University.

The panic over *Dungeons & Dragons* subsided as Grunge

music became a more popular pastime for America's youth. Academic studies have since shown that the game didn't contribute to more teen suicides, and criminologists point out that any amount of crime associate with *D & D* was negligible at best.

Kids who had to hide their twelve-sided dice from their parents in the 1980s are now parents who wish their kids would play *Dungeons & Dragons* rather than spend all day fixated on their phones.

# Oliver Stone and
# Alexander the Great

Oliver Stone is known for making epic historical and biographical movies (such as *JFK* and *The Doors*)that feature long runtimes and are successful at the box office. Many of Stone's films revolve around a specific historical personality and offer plenty of conspiracy theories along the way.

Although his 2004 biopic *Alexander* was short of conspiracy theories, it did hint that the Macedonian general and king was poisoned by his own subordinates. So where did Stone get this idea, and is it true?

Well, Oliver Stone's conspiracy theory regarding Alexander the Great's death was not original; it has actually circulated for over two thousand years.

Alexander III (Alexander the Great) was the king of the Greek-speaking kingdom of Macedon, who left his kingdom in 334 BC with his vast army. Within four years, he had conquered the Persian Empire and, along with it, most of the civilized world. Spurred on by a thirst for knowledge and war, Alexander led his men further east to the Indus River and the boundaries of India, until his men had had enough and wanted to go home. Alexander then set up court for his new empire in the ancient Mesopotamian capital of Babylon, where he lived until he died in 323 at the ripe age of thirty-two.

Alexander's death sent the Greek world into civil war as his generals fought for their piece of the pie. His only living child was a son he had with a non-Greek woman, which meant that most of Greek world would never have accepted him as king.

Almost immediately, Alexander's mother Olympias began spreading the story that Antipater, one of Alexander's trusted generals, had one of his sons poison Alexander. The Antipater conspiracy theory was documented by the first-century BC Greek historian, Diodorus, and the second-century AD Greek historian Arrian.

If it was written down then it must be true, right?

Writers, even historians who claim to be objective, still have opinions, which can sometimes turn into an agenda. Even ancient writers were guilty of having agendas—maybe even more so. Also, if one looks at the case logically, there was no reason for Antipater and his sons to have killed Alexander. They didn't try to usurp the empire when he died, and they didn't benefit from Alexander's death more than any of the other generals.

Finally, other sources, such as the second-century AD historian Plutarch, proclaimed that all stories that stated Antipater and his family were behind Alexander's death came from Olympias. The latter was trying to put her grandson, Alexander's son, on the throne which would give her the ultimate power.

If Alexander the Great wasn't poisoned, how did he die?

The sources all agree that he died from a fever, which was not uncommon during that period in history. Alexander was a general who personally led his troops into battle, and he incurred several serious injuries as a result. In an era long before antibiotic medication existed, there is a very high probability that Alexander received an infection from one of his wounds that turned into a fever and killed him.

Oliver Stone is a filmmaker not a historian. Death by assassination definitely sounds more interesting in a movie than an infection, right?

# Don't Touch My Sacred Cow

Languages are a funny thing. Among all the rules of grammar, syntax, and spelling, there are also regional dialects, vernaculars, and colloquialisms that can sometimes make understanding your native language (never mind a foreign one) difficult at times. The truth is we use slang terms and colloquial idioms every day and don't even know were doing it.

For instance, take the phrase "sacred cow."

If you are a native English speaker, or fluent in English, you've certainly heard this phrase and probably used it yourself, hopefully correctly! The term "sacred cow" is often used in the context of government and politics. For example, in America the Social Security system is often referred to as a "sacred cow" that neither the Democrats nor the Republicans will touch. In Britain, the National Healthcare System is also often referred to as a "sacred cow." You can probably gather from the context that the term refers to something (often a governmental institution or program) that, for whatever reasons, cannot be modified, altered, or cut.

You're probably thinking: "Fair enough, but what's all that have to do with a cow?"

It is difficult to say for sure when the phrase "sacred cow" entered the English language, but it was probably either in the late 1700s or early 1800s in England.

India was a collection of kingdoms when the British East India Company began setting up bases throughout the country in the 1600s. The British East India Company was subsidized by the British government and so the British military worked alongside company merchants to establish control of the country. After the Sepoy, or Indian Rebellion of 1857, control over India passed officially to the British crown. By that point, the connections between the countries were extensive and thousands of British citizens had lived in India and brought back tales of the country's unique religious beliefs.

One of those was the Hindu belief that cows are sacred animals.

Pious Hindus abstain from eating beef and will do whatever they can to avoid hurting a cow, which is why whenever you see a news report, film, or television show from India, there's always almost at least one cow running around in traffic.

So, the phrase probably first saw usage in England before making its way over to the United States and other English-speaking countries in the 1800s.

Another theory is that an Indian living in Janesville, Wisconsin sent a letter home to India in 1854 that was published in *The Calcutta Times*. In the letter, the pious Hindu Wady Jahed wrote about some of the curious customs of his American hosts, particularly how they ate the flesh of the sacred cow. He closed his letter with "Kiss the Sacred Cow for Me."

It's funny how some things make it into the English language.

# When *Terminator* Becomes Real

In the films and television shows belonging to the *Terminator* franchise, the world is eventually turned into an apocalyptic wasteland by computers and robots bent on the destruction of humanity. Those who survive the computers' initial onslaught are forced to live underground and form human resistance groups. The humans eventually discover time travel and repeatedly send missions to the past to try to stop the computers before they launch their initial attack.

This theme was also repeated in the *Matrix* series and the *Blade Runner* series, albeit with different details.

Although these movies exist purely in the realm of science fiction, like most good science fiction, they are based on some scientific reality. In the case of the *Terminator* and *Matrix* franchises, the scientific theory that they are based on is known as *singularity*. Simply put, singularity is defined as a point where technology has advanced so much that it can no longer be controlled. More specifically, it refers to the point at which Artificial Intelligence (AI) becomes "self-aware" and no longer needs humans to carry out programs and other functions. In theory, AI can then create other programs, which in turn can replicate themselves and so on and so on. Essentially, we'd be looking at a new life-form.

I'm sure you can see the dilemmas that singularity may present, and so too did the late scientist Stephen Hawking and inventor/entrepreneur Elon Musk. The new AI life-form would still have the logic of its computer lineage, but it would be imbued with a newfound desire to protect its life at all costs. It could see humans as both a threat to its life and unnecessary for its continued existence.

That's when it starts building killer robots to go after us!

Not all agree that singularity is inevitable, though. Psychologist Steven Pinker and philosopher John Searle argue that computers will never be able to reach singularity because they aren't imbued with a human mind, while others have similarly argued that singularity will never happen because AI lacks a soul.

But none of singularity's detractors are scientists.

It appears that the true question is not *if* singularity will happen, but what will it look like when it *does* happen?

Will we all be placed into vessels in order for a giant mainframe to use our bodily fluids for power? Will anthropomorphic killer robots be unleashed on the world the instant AI becomes self-aware? Or will the AI look just like us and develop feelings and be known as "skin jobs?"

The reality is that it probably won't be as cool as any of these examples. When AI becomes self-aware, it will still need the help of humans to carry out many of its functions. Since we already have a certain amount of AI in our lives, many experts argue that the change will probably just make things run much more efficiently and that we shouldn't worry about anything.

Killer robots make for better fiction, right?

# The Deadliest Comet

In all of recorded human history (about five thousand years) there are no cases of an asteroid, meteorite, or comet definitely killing anyone. There are times when pieces of these celestial bodies have entered the atmosphere, and there is one case where a meteorite *may* have killed a couple of people in Siberia in 1908, but those deaths are unconfirmed.

There have been plenty of movies that detail the destruction such an impact would cause on Earth, and there is little doubt that if something did hit, it would cause floods, earthquakes, and civil unrest. And if the object was big enough, it could wipe out all life on the planet.

Most experts say the chances of something hitting us directly are remote, so we shouldn't be worried.

But what about the power of a comet to kill indirectly?

On March 26, 1997, members of the San Diego County, California Sheriff's Department responded to a welfare check at a residence known to house a number of eccentric individuals. When they arrived on the scene, they found thirty-nine men and women between the ages of twenty-six and seventy-two dead from suicide by poisoning. The macabre scene became more bizarre as investigators looked around. All of the dead, male and female, were dressed in black tracksuits with Nike shoes. They all also had their heads shaved, and it was later learned that many of the men were castrated.

The investigators soon found a videotape explaining what had happened, and two survivors came forward. The dead were part of a religious cult, known as "Heaven's Gate," who believed that by committing suicide they would shed their bodies and catch a ride on a spaceship that was following the Hale-Bopp comet.

Needless to say, the world was shocked.

By 1997, religious cults were nothing new to America and the Heaven's Gate cult mass suicide was not the largest in history—nine hundred eighteen people had committed suicide or were murdered as part of the Jonestown, Guyana/People's Temple massacre in 1978. But the Heaven's Gate mass suicide seemed bizarre because of its leaders and their ideology.

The Heaven's Gate was led by Marshal Applewhite (known as "Do," born in 1931) and fifty-seven-year-old Bonnie Nettles ("Ti," born in 1927). The way in which the two met is a bit murky, although many sources say that Applewhite was a patient at a mental hospital where Nettles was a nurse in the 1970s. By the mid-1970s the pair had formulated a complex theology that combined elements of Christianity, theosophy, and New Age Ufology. By the late 1970s, the two had amassed a small following of former hippies and disaffected youth and began living communally as a traditional cult.

Ti and Do told their followers that their bodies were mere vessels and that after they "ascended" by acquiring more knowledge, they would shed their bodies and live as the aliens do: asexual and without any need for food, water, or even air.

To demonstrate his commitment to the cause, Do had himself castrated at a cheap, and no doubt less-than-reputable, clinic in Tijuana, Mexico.

As extreme as that may sound, extreme acts are part and parcel of most cults. It not only showed followers that Do was willing to walk the walk, but it also served as a litmus test for the true believers. The men who followed suit by also getting castrated became part of Do's inner circle.

When Ti died of cancer in 1985, it only seemed to push the Heaven's Gate into deeper cult territory. As the 1990s rolled around and the year 2000 loomed on the horizon, it began to take on the trappings of a millennial cult.

Millennial cults were somewhat common in the 1990s, and fear of comets passing by the Earth has also been recorded for centuries. But when those two things mixed with one of the most bizarre cults in modern history, they created a toxic cocktail.

On March 20, 1997, Do recorded a video-taped confession where he explained that he and twenty other male members and eighteen female members of Heaven's Gate needed to shed their bodies to catch a ride behind Hale-Bopp. Then, beginning on March 22, in two groups fifteen and one group of nine, members began ingesting deadly amounts of phenobarbital. As they dozed off, they put plastic bags over their heads to make sure the job was done.

They were all going to catch that ride on the mother ship.

The result was the largest mass suicide to occur on American soil and also the deadliest comet—which never even hit the Earth.

# Colonel Hogan's Secret Life

Earlier in this book, we took a look at some of the interesting but little-known facts about the popular American sitcom *Hogan's Heroes*. I also mentioned that there was another story to be told about the show's star, Robert "Bob" Crane, who played Colonel Hogan. While *Hogan's Heroes* was on the air, Crane was in his early forties, married, and the father of five children. He had divorced his first wife and remarried in 1970, but everything else seemed to be going great for Crane—he was making good money on the show and was also forging important contacts in Hollywood.

But Crane was feeding a dark side.

It was well known by most who knew Crane that he was a ladies' man. Thanks to his all-American looks and a confidence that was refined while he was a radio DJ in the 1950s, Crane had a way with women. When Crane married for the first time in 1948, he didn't let a wedding ring slow down his womanizing. Nor did his second marriage change his ways. In fact, while he starred on *Hogan's Heroes*, his womanizing went into overdrive—eventually dipping into the realm of perversity, and ultimately costing him his life.

The combination of Crane's fame from the show, and the loosening of sexual mores during the 1960s, meant that he always had a sizable pool of willing women to play with. But, as with any other addiction, Crane began to grow bored with normal sex.

Crane's boredom was cured when he met Henry Carpenter, a sales manager for Sony Electronics, after *Hogan's Heroes* was cancelled. Carpenter was immediately impressed with his new friend's star-studded background, as well as his ability to score with the chicks. For his part, Crane enjoyed having a sidekick, but more importantly, he found a use for Carpenter's knowledge of electronics.

He would have Carpenter secretly film the two men's sexual encounters with women.

Even within the sexually libertine circles of Hollywood, Crane kept his sexual addiction a secret for the most part. The women he had sex with were never involved in Hollywood, which allowed Crane to separate his personal and professional lives. Crane's compartmentalization of his life also made things difficult for the police when they found his body in a Scottsdale, Arizona on June 29, 1978.

Crane's body and head had been severely beaten with a blunt object. As the police searched through the blood-soaked room for a weapon, which they never found, they discovered a collection of videotapes. The police were shocked to learn that the tapes were actually homemade pornos of Colonel Hogan and another man performing a variety of different sexual acts on several different women. After doing a little detective work, the police learned the identity of Henry Carpenter.

Carpenter admitted that he was in the Phoenix area, saw Crane around the time of the murder, and that he had Colonel Hogan were "tag team" partners. But he was adamant that he had nothing to do with Crane's death. The police were skeptical, but they had no real evidence to charge him.

The case went cold but was finally reopened in 1992. Carpenter was charged with murder and went on trial in 1994 but was acquitted. In addition to a lack of evidence tying Carpenter to the crime, there was a whole slew of other potential killers: Any number of the women in the videos may have feared being exposed to the point of murder, not to mention an angry husband could also have done the deed.

Besides having a weak physical case against Carpenter, the prosecution's motive was equally flimsy. They implied that Carpenter had a homosexual crush on Hogan and killed him out of jealousy.

Carpenter died in 1998, having denied murdering Crane until the end. A DNA test of blood found in Carpenter's rental car at the time was inconclusive, which means that theories about Crane's murder will also forever remain a mystery.

One thing is for sure though, Colonel Hogan's dark side had something to do with his death.

# It's Raining Fish

Since ancient times, people have recorded the bizarre phenomenon of fish, frogs, and other animals raining down from the skies. Yes, we are talking about it literally raining animals. This phenomenon has been recorded on nearly every continent and has been witnessed by thousands of people. The event often, but not always, takes place after a rainstorm and usually involves aquatic animals falling from the sky onto unsuspecting people. Sometimes only a few dozen animals will fall over an area of just a few square feet. Often, however, hundreds of creatures fall over a space of a few city blocks.

The community of Yoro, Honduras has been afflicted by falling fish so many times over the last century that they began hosting an annual celebration of the strange occurrence—Lluvia de Peces, or "Rain of Fish."

The Greeks believed that these animals actually "grew" from the ground after heavy rains, which is not so illogical when you consider that worms do seem to grow from the ground after a rain. But we know more about science today and such a thing isn't possible. So then, what is the science behind these occurrences?

Most scientists who have attempted to tackle this vexing problem point out that most cases involve aquatic or semi-aquatic animals and take place after a rain or thunderstorm. They argue that a whirlwind or tornado simply picks the animals up from a nearby body of water and then deposits them on some frightened, unsuspecting people.

This sounds like a plausible theory. But how does it explain spiders dropping from the sky in Goulburn, New South Wales, Australia in 2015, or the fact that many of these cases have taken place in locations where there is little to no tornadic activity?

It seems like this will be another mystery that will remain unsolved.

# Getting Above
# the Mendoza Line

The sport of baseball has come a long way since its creation more than one hundred fifty years ago in the United States. After staying within the confines of America for most of its life, the sport sprang forth from its homeland after World War II and is now the most popular sport in such countries as Japan, South Korea, Venezuela, and the Dominican Republic. It is also among the more popular sports in Mexico, many of the non-British Caribbean countries, and Australia, and is gaining in popularity throughout Europe.

Fans of baseball are attracted to the unique combination of skills, athleticism, and strategy that it requires of its players, as well as its reliance on statistics. Perhaps more than any other sport, baseball is a game of stats. Batting average, ERA, OPS, and WHIP are just some of the metrics used to determine a player's value.

But what about the "Mendoza Line"?

If you've watched any amount of baseball in the last forty years, you've probably heard the Mendoza Line used as a stat; but the thing is, it's not an actual stat!

The term Mendoza Line actually began as a joke and as a reference to Mexican professional baseball player Mario Mendoza's lack of batting prowess. Mendoza was a shortstop who originally played in the Mexican professional leagues before becoming what is known as a "journeyman" in Major League Baseball, playing for the Pittsburgh Pirates, Seattle Mariners, and Texas Rangers in the 1970s and early 1980s, before returning to Mexico to finish his playing career.

Mendoza was known as an excellent fielder, but he was never a very good Major League hitter, and he had a difficult time batting about a .200 average, which is not very good in baseball. The phrase first surfaced during the 1979 Major League season when some of Mendoza's teammates told Kansas City Royals' slugger and Hall of Famer George Brett that if he didn't turn his season around, he'd be in danger of sinking "below the Mendoza Line."

Baseball is a sport of practical jokers—Brett was never in any danger of batting below .200, but the joke caught on and was picked up by Chris Berman.

If you're an American, you're probably familiar with Chris Berman, the ESPN announcer and personality who brings a bit of humor to his analysis and broadcasts. In 1979, most people had not heard of Berman, in fact, most people had not heard of ESPN either—it was a new network that year and wasn't available most places. But Berman began using the term "Mendoza Line" that year, not only to refer to Mario Mendoza's lack of hitting luck in the Majors, but also to refer to the .200 average in general.

By the mid-1980s, sports announcers all over the United States were regularly referring .200 as the Mendoza Line and now, with baseball's increasing international popularity, it can be heard uttered in Asia, Latin America, and even Europe.

Although the term began as a big joke on Mario Mendoza, he ended up having the last laugh. His career Major League Baseball average was .215.

# The Celebrity Cannibal

The annals of history are filled with many celebrity criminals. Most celebrity criminals attained their fame after being caught and have only been able to enjoy their status from behind bars. But this is not always the case. One of the most bizarre criminal cases in history involved a Japanese man named Issei Sagawa, who brutally murdered and cannibalized a woman. Although his crime is certainly shocking, what makes this case even more shocking is the fact that he was actually released from confinement and got to enjoy fame (or infamy) from it as a free man.

Issei Sagawa was never quite right in the head.

Sagawa was born a premature baby in Kobe, Japan in 1949 to a family of means and connections. From an early age, Sagawa knew that he wasn't like the other kids. When he was in the first grade, Sagawa began seeing the other kids not simply as other children, but as food! To him, the urge to commit cannibalism was/is quite natural as he said in interview:

"I can't fathom why everyone doesn't feel this urge to eat, to consume, other people."

For Sagawa, cannibalism and sexuality were intertwined and part of a fetish he continually fed internally, although he didn't act on it in real life. To satisfy his twisted sexual desires, Sagawa sexually assaulted his family's dog and then attacked a German woman with the intent to eat her. Although he was caught before he could kill the woman, the failure taught Sagawa how to commit a crime and allowed him to establish an M.O.

At four feet nine inches, Sagawa was very short (even for a Japanese person) and not particularly good looking. His physical qualities were always a source of pain for him and they are what drove him to strike out at society. He was particularly attracted to tall, good looking women and he wanted to gain those qualities through cannibalism.

Sagawa continued to put up a good public front and was able to secure a spot as a doctoral candidate in poetry at Paris' Sorbonne University in 1977.

The first couple of years went well for Sagawa, but in June of 1981, he couldn't wait anymore.

He had to eat someone.

He chose fellow student Renée Hartevelt as his victim. Hartevelt was everything Sagawa was looking for and everything he wasn't: tall, attractive, and sure of herself. Sagawa invited Hartevelt to his apartment for dinner and to study. As the night progressed and the pair had a few drinks, the would-be cannibal jumped into action. He pulled out a hunting rifle from his secret spot and prepared to shoot her from behind but froze at the moment of truth.

"[It] made me even more hysterical and I knew that I simply had to kill her," he later said about failing to murder his classmate.

Sagawa then invited Hartevelt over on the evening of June 11, 1981. Being familiar with the seemingly polite and gentlemanly Japanese student, she readily accepted.

This time Sagawa didn't freeze.

He shot Hartevelt from behind, almost immediately raped her corpse, and then proceeded to slice pieces of flesh from her buttocks and other parts of her body. He continued to feast on Hartevelt for several days and was finally caught when he attempted to throw her remains in a lake. Sagawa confessed to murdering Hartevelt and cannibalizing her body. The only question now should have been not if he would go to prison, but how long he'd spend there.

But justice has a strange way of working in some nations.

The judge found Sagawa legally insane and therefore not liable for the crime under French law. He spent short time in a mental institution and was deported to Japan where many believed he would spend the rest of his life in a mental hospital. But since he hadn't been convicted of any crime in France, there was little that could be done to Sagawa under Japanese law.

He simply signed himself out of the hospital and walked into Japanese society a free man.

The case caused just as much of a stir in Japan as it did in France, and most Japanese were sickened by Sagawa's attack. But Japanese culture is such that following societal laws is perceived as a virtue and there is a high degree of trust, so the cannibal's life was never seriously threatened by vigilantes. He was free to live openly, gave plenty of interviews, wrote some columns, and even did a little acting.

As the 2000s came though, Issei Sagawa's celebrity status began to wane considerably. A young or even middle-aged cannibal might be interesting, or even sexy to some, but an elderly cannibal is just plain creepy. He now lives on public assistance, but still gives interviews to those willing to listen. And according to a 2017 interview he gave, his cannibalistic impulses continue to be strong in his old age.

"The desire to eat people becomes so intense around June when women start wearing less and showing more skin," Sagawa said. "Just today, I saw a girl with a really nice derrière on my way to the train station. When I see things like that, I think about wanting to eat someone again before I die."

Hopefully for the women of Japan, he's too old to pull off another attack.

# Mouthless Moths

The animal kingdom is full of many strange animals that can be found on nearly every corner of the planet. If you live in North America, chances are you've seen one of these strange animals at some point in your life, probably during the summer months.

The Luna Moth is a large green moth that can be found from Alaska down to southern Mexico. Its lime-green color makes it nice to behold, and its four-and-a-half to seven-inch span certainly makes it noticeable. But the thing that makes the Luna Moth one of the strangest creatures in the animal kingdom is that it doesn't have a mouth.

Well, it does actually have a mouth, it just doesn't use it. If only that were the case with some people! One can only dream. But let's get back to the Luna Moth.

Luna Moths do have mouths, but they are nonfunctioning "vestigial" organs. Many animals, including us humans, have vestigial organs. In order to understand what a vestigial organ is, just consider the origin of the word—vestigial comes from "vestige," which refers to something that is left over or behind. Therefore, in animals, vestigial organs refer to organs that no longer have a practical function because the species has evolved past the point of needing or using them. The appendix is an example in humans, while the dewclaw is an example in domestic dogs.

I know what you're thinking: How could a mouth be a vestigial organ for *any* animal?

The answer comes down to the very short and diverse life cycle of a Luna Moth.

Like all butterflies and moths, the Luna Moth lives most of its life before becoming a fully-grown moth. A Luna Moth will spend about two weeks as an egg, two months as a larvae (caterpillar), and ninth months as a pupae before entering the world as the winged adult that we see flying around.

Then after a week, it dies.

When the Luna Moth is a caterpillar it consumes enough food for the rest of its life cycle. It stores the energy it needs for its adulthood as fat but doesn't need to eat anymore. As an adult, the Luna Moth's only purpose is to reproduce.

Then it dies, presumably happy.

# Which Chupacabra?

In terms of cryptozoology—the study of "hidden" or as of yet undiscovered animal species—the chupacabra occupies a special place due to the wide range of its sightings and the varied nature of its description. The name itself even sets it apart from most other questionable creatures of the dark: Chupacabra literally means "goat sucker" in Spanish; sightings of the creature are often accompanied by dead farm animals that have had all, or nearly all. the blood sucked from their bodies. But as sightings of this creature increased over the last twenty-five years, it turned out there were actually two different creatures named chupacabra.

Or maybe it was the same creature and it somehow evolved?

The story of the chupacabra begins in the remote areas of the Puerto Rican highlands in 1995. It was during that year when farmers began finding their prized goats dead and drained of all blood. The only evidence that pointed toward anything were two puncture marks left on the animals' necks, which looked eerily like something out of a vampire movie.

Word of the attacks began to spread and finally sightings of the goat suckers were reported. The chupacabra was described as a bipedal creature, about four to five feet tall, with scaly skin, a head that resembles that of a "gray alien," and long, claw-like fingers. Numerous sightings of the scary creature were reported around Puerto Rico and then in other

Latin American countries throughout the 1990s, but by the early 2000s the sightings began to evolve.

Goats, chickens, and other domestic animals were still being found drained of all their blood in a number of different Latin American locations, but there were less and less reports of bipedal creatures to go along with the attacks. Instead, witnesses began reporting vicious looking canine creatures.

People began regularly sighting the new chupacabras north of the Rio Grande River.

Theories about the newer chupacabra sightings ran the gamut from logical to absurd: Some argued that the creatures sighted were probably just sick coyotes, while others thought the chupacabras were a new hybrid species, or worse, a science experiment gone wrong that had escaped from a lab.

Finally, by the late 2000s, chupacabra corpses began turning up in Texas that could be professionally tested in labs. All of the tests revealed that the chupacabras were either domestic dogs, coyotes, wolves, or a mixture of the three. Experts believe that the bizarre appearance of the creatures is primarily the result of mange or other infections.

Nothing otherworldly.

As for the reports of farm animals drained of all blood . . . well, experts have pointed out that in most cases this was exaggerated. They say that the animals lost plenty of blood, but that it was all caused by predators feeding on them. Other experts have pointed out that when mammals die the blood goes to the extremities, giving the impression that they no longer have blood.

And how did the chupacabra evolve from a bipedal creature to a canine?

Well, the original cases in Puerto Rico began with a single eyewitness. Her testimony got front-page newspaper attention in the American commonwealth and became an urban legend in the early days of the World Wide Web. So, skeptics believe that the mystery of the chupacabra has been solved.

Or has it?

Some point out that mange doesn't explain all of the mutated-looking canines found in Texas, and they suggest that they are possibly a new species created by continued crossbreeding between coyotes and domestic dogs. The logical explanations also don't necessarily explain how most of the farm animals were killed. Though not all of their blood was sucked out, the dead animals weren't eaten in typical canine fashion.

These unanswered questions have led some to conclude that although the original Puerto Rican chupacabra sightings were probably a hoax, the later ones were based on valid creature sightings that were/are possibly a hybrid canine species.

# The Language of Love, in Eastern Europe

No doubt, you are familiar with the term "Romance language." You probably also know that Italian, French, and Spanish are considered Romance languages because they sound so nice and romantic, right?

Wrong!

Italian, French, Spanish, and Portuguese are called Romance languages because they are directly descended from the ancient Latin language, which was the language of Rome. Sure, those languages may sound real nice and knowing them a little may help you score some points on a date, but they have more to do with gladiatorial combat, crucifixions, and Stoic philosophers than they do with guys trying to woo women.

And you may also be surprised to learn that the eastern European language Romanian is also a Romance language.

In ancient times, the area of Europe that is today called Romania was known as Dacia. The Dacians were a brave and proud people who spoke an Indo-European language that is now extinct. They had established a powerful and wealthy kingdom by the first century AD, but the ever-expanding Romans coveted Dacian land and their many goldmines.

The Roman Emperor Trajan destroyed the Dacian Kingdom in AD 105, and from that point on the Dacian people became heavily "Romanized." The Dacians accepted Roman culture, many of their men joined the Roman Army, and the elites began using the Latin language.

By the time the Western Roman Empire collapsed in AD 476, the various regions of the empire had already been fairly autonomous and their cultures and languages were influenced by their neighbors: German language and culture influenced French, Spanish, and Portuguese to varying extents, while Romanian was influenced by its Slavic neighbors.

Because of its Slavic influence and the fact that speakers of Romanian have accents that sound "Eastern European" to those not familiar with it, it is usually not thought of as a Romance language. But a closer look at some of the words shows it is. For instance, "bine" means good in Romanian, while in Spanish it is "bien" and in Italian it is "bene." There are, of course, several more examples of cognate words, but it is also important to know (not to get too nerdy) that the basic syntax and morphology of Romanian is also similar to the other Romance languages.

The point is, that in the middle of the former Eastern Bloc, in the midst of millions of stoic Slavic-speaking peoples, is a group of people who speak a language closely related to Italian, French, and Spanish. So, the next time you want to impress your date, learn a little Romanian and find a bottle of nice Romanian *vin*.

It might earn you some points.

# A Radioactive Film

The 1956 film *The Conqueror* is often dismissed by movie critics as an attempt by John Wayne to expand his image and repertoire. If you aren't familiar with the film, it stars the popular actor as the legendary Mongol leader Genghis Khan. Yes, "The Duke." That John Wayne.

The film was produced by legendary playboy Howard Hughes, who was willing to spend a great deal of his fortune to make it a hit. He paid big bucks to get John Wayne to put his cowboy boots aside and to put on a silly-looking Fu Manchu mustache.

Once Hughes got his leading man, he moved production to the mountains and deserts of southern Utah. Many of the scenes were shot near the town of St. George, Utah, about one hundred thirty-seven miles downwind from the Nevada Test Site (NTS), which is where the U.S. military tested its nuclear weapons in the 1950s and 1960s.

The testing didn't stop while *The Conqueror* was being filmed.

Once location filming wrapped up in Utah, the ever-eccentric and obsessive Hughes then had several tons of Utah dirt delivered to the Hollywood studio where the final scenes were filmed. Although *The Conqueror* was panned by most critics, it did well at the box office thanks to the popularity of The Duke.

But then, people started getting sick.

Director Dick Powell died of cancer in early 1963, and star Pedro Armendáriz took his own life in June of 1963 after fighting kidney cancer for three years. The list of doomed stars and production members continues on: Leading lady Susan Howard died of brain cancer in 1975, star Agnes Moorhead succumbed to uterine cancer in 1974, star John Hoyt died of lung cancer in 1991, and leading man Wayne died of stomach cancer in 1979. Of the two hundred twenty cast and crew members who worked on the movie at the St. George location, ninety-one developed some form of cancer and forty-six people died of the disease.

Those are certainly shocking numbers. Skeptics, however, point out that a majority of the cast and crew smoked cigarettes.

Even so, the number of cancer cases associated with *The Conqueror* is higher than for any other known movie.

Hughes reportedly also felt remorse for his role in the situation. He bought all of the prints of the film, which effectively took it out of circulation until after his death. When the film began appearing on television in the 1980s, viewers were amused by Wayne's phony mustache and the fact that he didn't try to change his accent for the role. That amusement, though, turned to bemusement when details about the film set's detrimental impact on the health of the cast and crew were revealed.

Whether or not nuclear weapons testing led to the unnatural deaths of the cast and crew of *The Conqueror* will never be known for sure, but it is interesting that the major nuclear powers of the world agreed to ban aboveground nuclear weapons testing in 1963.

# Animals That Don't Age

Since the dawn of history, the idea of immortality has intrigued humans—sometimes to the point of obsession. Myths from every corner of the globe and every period in history tell of gods and goddesses who live forever and human heroes who strive to possess that knowledge and ability. Today, many of the current major religions of the world offer the reward of eternal life for pious believers, which is a testament to man's will to overcome death.

With the advent of modern science, some scientists began examining the biology behind aging. In the process, they have developed theories that claim to slow the effects of aging. There is no doubt that modern medicine has vastly prolonged human lives over the last one hundred years, and as medical technology progresses even more, the average human life span will no doubt also increase. Some scientists believe that if medical science continues to progress as its current rate, over the next few decades, people will begin to regularly live to one hundred and we will even see the first person live to one hundred fifty.

But that isn't good enough for some people who want to live eternally, or at least indefinitely.

No one at this point believes that humans can become indestructible, but some believe—based on examples from nature—that senescence (biological aging) can be massively retarded or even stopped. This may sound strange, but a closer look reveals that there is some truth to the theory.

The small freshwater class of organisms known as hydras are believed to be biologically immortal. Hydras have no brain, muscles, or vertebrae, and are therefore susceptible to death in a number of ways. But they have incredible regenerative abilities. The hydra's regenerative abilities, which allow it to recover quickly from injuries, are believed to be connected to their lack of aging.

The *Turritopsis dohrnii* (or immortal jellyfish) is also believed to be another animal that doesn't age. In fact, the immortal jellyfish has the unique ability to retard its life span by returning to the polyp stage when it is faced with adverse conditions such as starvation or extreme changes in temperature.

Other animals that have displayed a "negligible senescence" include different species of tortoises, sharks, and rockfish, all of which are believed to have the ability to live two hundred years or more.

What are the long-term implications for humanity? Scientists have been examining hydras and immortal jellyfish in order to determine if something can be taken from those animals to help slow the aging process in humans. At this point, taking action to extend life is still theoretical, but experiments may begin in the future where humans are injected with hydra cells.

The time for experimentation is probably closer than you think.

# As Rich as Croesus

You've probably heard the phrase "He's as rich as Croesus" at some point in your life and didn't give it much attention. After all, there are so many phrases and sayings that it's hard to keep up with them. But this one is important because it has to do with the money, or the lack of it, in your pocket.

You see, Croesus was a real person, and he very well could have been the richest man in the world during his lifetime.

Croesus was the king of the ancient Kingdom of Lydia (located in what is now central Turkey) from about 560 to the 540s BC. He was known for a lot of things. But, above all, he was known for putting on ostentatious displays of wealth. In fact, he liked to show off his wealth so much that he'd probably make rappers blush. According to Greek historian Herodotus, Croesus donated a large supply of gold, silver, and animals to the Oracle of Delphi in Greece in order to get a reading of the signs that were in his favor.

Talk about buying influence!

Croesus was the beneficiary of a wealthy kingdom that was created by some pretty forward-thinking rulers, at least in terms of economics. The capital city of Lydia, called Sardis, was located on the Pactolus River. The river was a source of electrum, a naturally occurring gold-silver alloy that could be traded as is or refined to separate the metals.

The Lydians preferred to separate the gold and silver and mint coins. Since we live in a society where paper and coin currency is ubiquitous, the use of coins for currency may not seem like a big deal. During the time of Croesus, however, it was actually a revolutionary step in world economics. Though gold and silver had been used in trade before the Lydians, they had assumed the form of clumsy, heavy ingots or dust. People before the Lydians, such as the Egyptians, had standardized prices for certain things, but they never had a standardized *currency*. The Lydians took the idea of standardized price and combined it with the inherent value of gold and silver to make the first circulating coins in the world. Lydian coins were standardized in basic weight and given specific values, thereby making all transactions simple and fairly honest.

Although the Kingdom of Lydia was conquered by the Persians and Croesus was probably killed, the conquerors continued the use of coins as currency and spread the idea throughout the Near East.

The Greeks, who were already quite familiar with the Lydians, also began using coins as currency by the sixth century BC, although the values differed from city-state to city-state.

By the time Alexander the Great conquered the Persians in 330 BC, coins used as currency was standard in most kingdoms and city-states in the Mediterranean and the Near East. The acceptance of coins for currency made things easy for the Romans when they took over the entire region in the first century BC—they simply adopted the existing economic system and gave it a different name.

None of this would've been possible, though, without the efforts of Croesus and the Lydians. As for paper money, that's a different story. . .

# The Dead Mountain

When a group of nine friends from the Ural Polytechnical Institute in the former Soviet Union decided to go hiking and skiing in the nearby Ural Mountains in early February of 1959, it seemed like a routine trip that many had done before. They would hike into the mountains and camp on the east shoulder of Kholat Syakhl, which translates into English as "Dead Mountain." The students happily left for their trip. But something absolutely strange, frightening, and unexplainable happened during February 1 and 2.

Whatever it was, it left all nine of the students dead!

The seven young men and two young women were led by Igor Dyatlov, who organized the expedition in Yekaterinburg, a sleepy college town in the middle of Siberia. Dyatlov made sure to select individuals with winter hiking and skiing experience, and the group left the comfort of their dormitories on January 25. A male member turned back two days later due to illness. The remaining nine members then trekked into the Urals, never to be seen alive again.

When Dyatlov didn't check in with some friends on February 12, friends and family of the hikers put pressure on the government to send out search teams. The rugged terrain and weather hampered rescue operations, which commenced a week later. By February 26, the remains of the hikers' camp were located.

The discovery was as baffling as it was shocking.

The tent was found torn and abandoned on the side of the mountain. Further examination revealed that the tent had been cut open from the inside, and the hikers had apparently left most of their clothes in the tent. Dyatlov and four of his comrades were found nearly naked about sixteen hundred feet from the tent. It appeared that they had attempted to start a fire, while others may have tried walking back to the tent.

Months passed before the bodies of the final four hikers were discovered.

It was initially thought that the hikers died of hypothermia. Even experienced hikers can fall victim to this condition. When hypothermia hits it can make a person do strange things, such as taking off one's clothes. But a closer examination of the bodies revealed that hypothermia didn't claim the lives of all the hikers.

When the remaining four bodies were discovered after the spring thaw, the case took a creepy turn.

Three of the bodies showed signs of severe trauma to the head and body, which was ruled the cause of death. What could have done this?

Since 1959 was the Cold War era, the Soviet government quickly put a lock on the story by closing access to the area and by controlling all press releases. The government also came up with a credible explanation to dispel any conspiracy theories.

The earliest and most commonly held theory for the tragedy was that the hikers were the victim of an avalanche. This would explain some of the injuries three of the hikers suffered and could also possibly account for the tent's destruction. But there are holes in theory. The footprints leading away from tent showed a normal gait, not a group running frantically to escape an avalanche. Furthermore, avalanches are not common in that part of the Urals; Dyatlov and fellow hiker Semyon Zolotaryov were highly experienced and would not have camped in an avalanche-prone area.

Another logical theory that has been bandied about to explain the tragedy at the Dyatlov Pass was that the hikers encountered a "Katabatic wind." A Katabatic wind is a wind that blows down the face of a mountain. Those who believe this theory think that such a wind blew down the face of the Dead Mountain, covering the unsuspecting men and women in a snowy grave.

After these scientific theories, we start getting into the realm of the conspiratorial and paranormal.

Another group of hikers reported seeing strange-looking orange orbs in the skies about thirty miles from the Dead Mountain. The Soviet government initially censored those reports. But after the USSR collapsed in 1991, those reports were made public, leading many to think that the tragedy on the Dead Mountain may have been a Soviet military exercise gone wrong.

Others think it was a fatal alien encounter that was later covered up by the Soviet government.

Perhaps the strangest of all the theories, and the one I like best, is that the hikers were the victim of a vicious yeti/Abominable Snowman. But although there have been supposed sightings of Yeti creatures in the area of the Dyatlov Pass, and the local Mansi people have numerous folk legends about its existence, no footprints of any creature were found near the dead hikers.

So, it appears that the yeti has once again been unfairly charged with a crime!

It looks as though the mystery of the Dyatlov Pass will continue for the foreseeable future.

# I'm Just a Bill

If you're from Generation X or even Generation Y, you no doubt remember Saturday morning cartoons with fondness. When cell phones were still uncommon and the only gaming system most people had in their homes featured poor graphics, kids would spend all Saturday morning glued to their TV watching *Captain Caveman, The Superfriends*, and other popular shows.

Although most of these cartoons were tame by today's standards, parent groups had a problem with what they thought was a lack of educational content, among other things. So, in an effort to be diplomatic, the networks began airing interstitial programing during the 1970s.

The most popular and famous of these was the series *Schoolhouse Rock!*

*Schoolhouse Rock!* first aired in 1973 and ran until 1985. It was later brought back in the 1990s and the 2000s. But those versions were a shadow of the original in both popularity and influence, so let's just focus on the original version. The series featured animated educational vignettes about math, science, grammar, and American history. Bob Dorough wrote and performed many of the songs, but one of the most memorable, "I'm Just a Bill," was written by Jack Frishberg and performed by Jack Sheldon.

The song follows the story of Bill, who (as the title of the song states) is just a bill, but he is hoping to someday become a law. The song then relates the process whereby a bill originates, faces a potential veto, and eventually becomes a law.

The song was as catchy as it was instructional.

But as popular and informative as *Schoolhouse Rock!* was, it couldn't survive the changing times. When the popularity of Saturday morning cartoons peaked in the mid-1980s, so too did the popularity and perceived need for educational programming. Parent groups became more concerned about Satanism in rock music and *Dungeons & Dragons* than they were about kids learning something on Saturday mornings. And when the original writers and performers of *Schoolhouse Rock!* tried to revive the series in the 1990s, they had such a smaller market for their shorts.

Saturday morning cartoons were a thing of the past and all the Gen Xers who watched *Schoolhouse Rock!* in the '70s and '80s were either starting families, in college, or trying to start grunge bands.

There was simply no market for the new *Schoolhouse Rock!*

But those of us who grew up watching Saturday morning cartoons will always have fond memories of *Schoolhouse Rock!* We also have YouTube.

# Iceberg Alley

The icy cold waters that stretch from the Davis Strait, which is between Greenland and the Canadian territory of Nanavut, down to the Grand Banks off the coasts of the Canadian provinces of Newfoundland and Nova Scotia, is known as the Atlantic Marine Ecozone. The waters were once home to abundant amounts of lobster, crab, shrimp, and cod, but overfishing has depleted the sea life. As a result, the area has not been a popular draw for fisherman over the last thirty years.

The Atlantic Marine Ecozone is also known for its many icebergs.

The icebergs rang in size from just a few feet long to several hundred feet long. At any given time, there can be hundreds floating in the water, which is how the Atlantic Marine Ecozone earned its nickname "Iceberg Alley." The icebergs form by breaking off from the glaciers of Greenland; they then slowly drift south for a few months to a few years. Often quite large in size, they are usually littered with rock and other grit from Greenland.

These icebergs made traversing the area hazardous for steamship liners in the late 1800s and early 1900s. Only the most experienced captains and the best ships were sent through the treacherous Iceberg Alley.

Captains like Edwin Smith and ships like the *Titanic*.

When the *Titanic* maneuvered through Iceberg Alley in 1912, it became part of history for the tragedy that happened after it hit a four-hundred-foot-long iceberg on April 14. After it sunk to the bottom of the Atlantic, taking with it the lives of more than fifteen hundred passengers, it was believed that the *Titanic's* remains would be a zone of death on the ocean floor. But, in a testament to the cycle of life, the ship has created a new mini-ecosystem within the Atlantic Marine Ecozone.

Aquatic algae and other deepwater organisms now call the remains of the *Titanic* their home. In fact, scientists believe that the process will become so thorough, one day soon very few visible remnants of the ship will exist.

# What Do Witches Have to Do with It?

There's a good chance that, at some point in your life, you've had a sensitive itch that you couldn't reach and bought some Tucks or Preparation H to make it go away. You may have been so impressed with how well the medicine did its job that you took the time to read the ingredients. After getting past some of the ingredients you couldn't pronounce, you eventually made it to "witch hazel."

"Witch hazel... what do witches have to do with that itch I couldn't reach?" you thought to yourself.

Well, witches have absolutely nothing to do with it.

Witch hazel is a genus of flowers from the family *Hamamelidaceae* that has been used as a natural remedy for inflammation for centuries by a number of different cultures. The American Indians used the native North American plant for a variety of rashes and other skin ailments, and when the Europeans arrived, they too learned of its medicinal properties. Witch hazel is applied topically to infected areas and is beneficial in treating diaper rash, eczema, and that itch you can't reach—hemorrhoids!

So, what do witches have to do with it?

Well, they actually have nothing at all to do the flowers of the *Hamamelidaceae* family.

The origin of the name can be traced back to the first Europeans who came in contact with it. During the seventeenth century, when the Puritans first learned of witch hazel, the English they spoke was a combination of Middle English and Modern English. In Middle English, "wyche" means "bend"; this is where most scholars believe witch hazel originally got its name. Not long after the Puritans discovered the flower, they quit using the word "wyche" to mean "bend." And the pronunciation gradually evolved to "witch."

The flower continued to be used as a home remedy for centuries until it became commercialized in more recent decades. But a funny thing happened: As witch hazel began to be sold commercially and also appeared as an active ingredient in over-the-counter medications, the New Age movement became popular. New Age "witches" turned to age-old natural remedies to concoct various "spells."

It was through the New Age movement's fascination with natural remedies that witch hazel began to be associated with witches in modern peoples' minds.

But now you know—witches have nothing to do with that terrible itch you can't reach.

# Canadians Call
# It Football Too

Have you ever noticed that Europeans get upset whenever an American refers to "football" as "soccer"? And how about the fact that Americans refer to their own most popular sport as "football" even though it isn't soccer? I'm not trying to confuse you here. This seems to be a legitimate concern for many in Europe, especially the British. For their part, Americans don't really care what other people think about their sports preferences.

But, to avoid confusion here, let's refer to "American football" by its technically correct name: "gridiron" or "football."

Gridiron evolved in the 1800s in North America out of soccer and rugby, which were imported by the British. Notice I said North America? Yes, that's because gridiron is the second most popular sport in Canada, right behind hockey. As much as Canadians may want to distance themselves from their neighbors south of their border, the reality is that they have as much in common with them, if not more, than they do with their British cousins across the pond.

In fact, the modern rules of gridiron football were first developed at McGill University in Montreal in the late 1800s and then adopted by schools and clubs in the United States.

The game then developed quickly in both countries to

resemble its current method of play. The field of play is a one-hundred-yard field divided into "yard markers," giving it a gridiron look (thus, the name). The ball is spherical, like in rugby, and the teams attempt to score by either running the ball into the end zones or kicking it through goalposts, also like in rugby. But that's where the similarities end.

Instead of constant play, gridiron play is divided into "downs" where the team with possession of the ball has three to four attempts to get a fresh set of downs. If the team in possession of the ball fails to get a new set of downs then the other teams gains possession. Six points are awarded for running the ball into the end zone (a touchdown), while either one point or three points are awarded for kicking the ball through the goalposts. Teams that score a touchdown can either attempt to get one "extra point" by kicking the ball through the goalposts or two "extra points" by getting the ball into the end zone on one play.

To a Brit who thinks gridiron is dumb or boring, the rules and play of a National Football League (NFL) game may look the same as that of a Canadian Football League (CFL) game. But to Americans and Canadians, they are quite different.

Both games use the same type of ball. They also advance the ball and score in similar fashion, and the length of the games are the same. Beyond that, however, there are some notable differences.

CFL teams field twelve men on a team at a time, while NFL teams only field eleven. The CFL fields are also slightly longer in the end zones and wider, which makes for quicker play. There are also only three downs per possession in the CFL versus four in the NFL, which creates higher scoring games and much more passing.

The goalposts are in the front of the end zones in the CFL, instead of in the back as they are in the NFL.

Scoring is pretty much the same in both leagues, except the CFL has a "single," which can be scored when the team kicking off kicks the ball through the end zone.

Because Canada is a much smaller country, the CFL is a much smaller league and generates much less revenue. The top CFL players earn about five hundred thousand dollars, which is great for the average Canadian or American, but nothing compared to their NFL counterparts. There are also only nine teams in the CFL, and the stadiums are much smaller than those in the NFL.

Because winter starts so early in much of Canada, especially in the plains and Rocky Mountain provinces, the CFL begins play in June and wraps up with the championship game (known as the Grey Cup) in late November. The early start also allows the CFL to pick up some fans south of the border since the NFL doesn't begin its regular season until early September.

There have been attempts, usually by American businessmen, to export gridiron from North America to other parts of the world, but they have largely failed. The NFL established a minor league in Europe that folded, and although there are minor leagues in several non-North American countries, they haven't generated very much interest. So, for the foreseeable future, gridiron—or football as Americans *and* Canadians like to call it—will stay primarily north of the Rio Grande.

# Steam Power in
# the Ancient World

The use of steam power is generally associated with the Industrial Revolution and the eighteenth and nineteenth centuries. Steam-powered ships and trains helped modernize and bring the world together. Before that, everything was fairly primitive, right?

Well, not exactly. Yes, the Industrial Revolution didn't begin until the 1700s. But the idea of steam power had been figured out, and forgotten, nearly two thousand years prior.

The idea to use steam, and therefore water, to power things is as ancient as it is logical. The ancients were around water every day and saw that its power was enough to make things move, and the most intelligent of them reasoned that if they could somehow make water move on command, then they could do things others only imagined!

The first man to develop serious hydropower theories was a Greek from Alexandria, Egypt named Ctesibius, who lived in the third century BC. Ctesibius was a member of the famed Museum of Alexandria and had access to the newly opened Library of Alexandria, which is where he got some of his invention ideas. He is credited with inventing a water-powered pipe organ and improving existing water clocks. Ctesibius' contributions to science extended beyond his own lifetime, however, as his inventions influenced later scientists to move forward with his ideas.

The Roman engineer Vitruvius (ca. 80-15 BC) was inspired by Ctesibius to create many military inventions and improvements in architecture, most notably central heating. But perhaps one of his most interesting experiments was with an early aeolipile, or steam engine.

The aeolipile was actually quite a simple device. It consisted of a radial steam turbine that was powered by two hollow tubes that connected it to a water container below it. The container was heated until steam was created, making the turbine move.

Although Vitruvius offered the first description of the aeolipile, the device is often more closely associated with another scientist from Alexandria, Hero of Alexandria (ca. AD 10-70). Besides the aeolipile, Hero invented a water-powered vending machine, a force pump, and several mechanical devices that were used in theaters.

Unfortunately, though, Hero's inventions never caught on enough to be widely distributed. It also didn't help that the Library of Alexandria was destroyed during the late Roman Empire or early Islamic Period in Egypt.

And there was also this little thing called the Dark Ages.

So, early experimentations with steam power were forgotten until the Early Modern Period. It is interesting to think of where we might be if the experiments of Vitruvius and Hero would have been improved instead of forgotten.

# The Kid Who Ended
# the Cold War

The Cold War was a time of great tension and fear in many parts of the world. The United States and the Soviet Union were engaged in an epic struggle for control of the world and, as a result, many smaller countries became proxies and were torn apart. Korea, Vietnam, Nicaragua, and Afghanistan were just some of the countries that the communist United Soviet Socialist Republic and the democratic-capitalist United States of America fought over in order to forward their agendas.

Although the war never came directly to the United States or the Soviet Union, there was a chance that either side would launch their large cache of intercontinental ballistic missiles. It was also possible that tensions in one of the proxy wars could escalate and lead to a large-scale conventional war.

The rhetoric by politicians on both sides didn't help either.

In a now-famous 1983 speech, American President Ronald Reagan described the Soviet Union as an "evil empire" that he wanted to bring down. Reagan's strategy to defeat the Soviet Union was to outspend them in military investments and to continue to support pro-American proxies in places like Central America. Still, the Soviets were able to meet the American challenge. Even after reformer Mikhail Gorbachev became the leader of the USSR in 1985, the situation continued.

But then, on May 28, 1987, an eighteen-year-old German amateur pilot named Mathias Rust changed everything when he literally flew his small Cessna plane under Soviet radars and landed in central Moscow near Red Square.

Mathias Rust wasn't very different from any other kid from West Germany, or the West in general, for that matter. He enjoyed music and hanging out with his friends, and didn't really think too much about long-term plans. Rust also wasn't very political. But he was concerned with the Cold War, which was a very real thing for Germans at that time.

Many German families were broken up when the country was partitioned into a democratic West Germany and a communist East Germany, and many Germans were later killed trying to escape the East.

All of this affected Rust very much as he grew up in Wedel, West Germany. He was also deeply moved by his grandparents' generation, who lost everything in World War II. So, Rust decided that he wanted to make a major statement about the Cold War, but he just didn't know how.

Until early 1987.

Rust had begun taking flying lessons that year and had logged about fifty hours of flying time when he decided to use that knowledge to make a bold statement to the world. He flew a small Cessna to Iceland and Norway before heading to Helsinki, Finland. From Helsinki, instead of heading south back to West Germany, Rust made the fateful and dangerous decision to fly into Soviet airspace. Remember, this was during the Cold War, so flying unauthorized into Soviet airspace could have been viewed as an act of war. Rust made the situation even more precarious when he ignored all radio contact with Soviet officials and flew low to the ground to avoid radar.

He also had the unexpected help of the Soviet military.

Soviet anti-aircraft batteries on the ground and fighter aircraft in the sky made contact with him on numerous occasions but would lose him before being given permission to engage. Rust kept plodding along in his Cessna until he made it to central Moscow, where he landed on the Bolshoy Moskvoretsky Bridge near Red Square. Tourists and locals alike were astonished by the situation, even more so when they learned Rust was from West Germany.

Rust was promptly arrested, tried, and convicted of a host of charges. He was given a four-year prison sentence but was released on August 3, 1988, after serving just over a year.

By the time Mathias Rust was released from prison, the geopolitical situation had changed radically. The Soviets were pulling out of Afghanistan, the United States had reduced its presence in Central America, and summits were being regularly held between Soviet and American leaders.

It was clear to people around the world that the Cold War was coming to an end.

And many historians and military analysists believe Mathias Rust played no small part in the matter. His flight to Moscow exposed fundamental problems in the Soviet air defense system and led to hundreds of military officers losing their jobs, the most since the Stalin purges of the 1930s and '40s.

Many believe that Rust's flight was little more than a teenager's prank, albeit a very elaborate one, but Rust contends to this day that he did it to help end the Cold War. Whether he intended to or not, Rust's flight certainly was a contributing factor in the collapse of the Iron Curtain.

# Who Knew Bigfoot
# Was a Snow Bird?

When one thinks of southern Florida, images of loud retirees from New York and New Jersey may come to mind. Or maybe you think of fishing off the shores of Key West. Or perhaps you're more of a nightlife person who enjoys dancing to a Latin beat.

All of these things are true aspects of southern Florida, but they represent such a small proportion of the overall land area. Not far from the hustle and bustle of metropolitan Miami, but still in Dade County, you'll find a world that is still wild and mostly untouched by civilization.

The Florida Everglades comprise the south central region of Florida and also extend into the metropolitan areas of Miami and Orlando. Wildlife abounds within the Everglades, or the "Glades" as locals call them. Although the Everglades are a swampy, jungle-type ecosystem, they are home to native populations of pumas, black bears, and a host of fish and fowl.

They are also reportedly the home of a Sasquatch-type creature named the "Skunk Ape."

Sightings of the Skunk Ape began in the late 1960s, and by 1974, sightings in suburban Dade County became so common that they made the local news. The Skunk Ape is described as a tall, hairy bipedal creature, much like Bigfoot. But, unlike Bigfoot, the Skunk Ape is usually accompanied by a rancid, sulfur-type smell, which is how it got the "skunk" part of its name. Apparently, Bigfoot's southern cousin is not too big on hygiene.

Sightings of the Skunk Ape continued through the 1980s and '90s and were reported more and more throughout the state. In 2000, the Sarasota Police Department received an anonymous letter with two photographs of what many people believe is the Skunk Ape, although skeptics think it is an orangutan. Skeptics believe that in most Skunk Ape sightings people actually are seeing *something*, but what they are usually seeing is one of the Sunshine State's many black bears.

But many cryptozoologists—people who study and document the existence of "hidden" animals or animals believed to be extinct—think that the Skunk Ape is actually a subspecies of animal that is related to the Bigfoot of the Pacific Northwest.

They believe that some Sasquatches prefer the warmer climate of sunny Florida.

As with the Skunk Ape's better known cousin from the northwest, sightings of the Florida Bigfoot ebb and flow. Curiously, they seem to go up when there is a new news report about the creature! Skunk Ape interest has increased with the popularity of YouTube, with people uploading their own takes on the creature. They can also watch the footage from a video of one taken by a hunter in the Everglades in 2000.

A few small expeditions have been launched to find the elusive Skunk Ape, but just like his cousin in the northwest, it looks like the Skunk Ape wants to be left alone.

# If Men Had to Give Birth. . .

Modern Western society is often highly sexually charged, pitting men against women. We can see these dynamics play out in our homes and families. No doubt, if you are a man reading this who has been in a serious relationship with a woman, you know how these things can happen. I'm not being judgmental here, just pointing out one of the realities of our world.

Oftentimes, domestic arguments arise over household chores, with both sides claiming the other isn't pulling his or her weight. Sometimes, the female partner will say something to the effect of, "If men had to give birth, things would be much different." Usually nothing more is said because it's just one of those things that really can't be answered.

Or can it?

Generally, we can look at other species in the animal kingdom to see how humans once acted before we became "civilized." Some examples can tell us a lot. Take, for instance, the seahorse. I'm sure you've seen pictures of a seahorse somewhere and know that it's actually a type of fish with a horse-like head. There are actually forty-five different species of seahorses in the genus *Hippocampus*, and they can be found in nearly every ocean in the world. Besides being interesting looking, seahorses have a fascinating trait that brings us back to our dilemma of the modern battle of the sexes.

Their males actually give birth.

Seahorse mating is much like other species of fish and the females do produce eggs. But once a female and male "court," the female deposits the eggs in a pouch in the male where they are fertilized and grow.

The seahorse mating ritual is actually quite complex, with the male and female changing colors and swimming together in what looks like a well-choreographed dance. The copulation doesn't happen until the end of the ritual. Once the eggs are successfully inserted in the male, he carries them for ten to forty-five days before giving birth to as many as several hundred baby seahorses.

The male can then breed again almost immediately.

Knowing this might not help men win arguments with their female partners...

But it is pretty neat to know that some males in the animal kingdom do know what it's like to give birth.

# A Criminal as Big as His Name

On August 8, 1963, a gang of well-organized criminals robbed the Royal Mail train headed from Glasgow, Scotland to London, England of £2.6 million, or about $3.2 million. This daring heist became known around the world as the "Great Train Robbery" and was the subject of numerous movies, books, and documentaries. Most of those involved in the crime were captured within about five years, served several years in prison, and were released by the late 1970s. From there, some became minor celebrities, while others went back to their lives of crime.

One of the robbers, Ronnie Biggs, just wouldn't give up; he kept fighting the system until he was an old man.

Ronnie Biggs' role in the Great Train Robbery was relatively minor and, for the most part, unsuccessful. He was supposed to work with an "insider" and move one train to another track, but when the insider was unable to do so, Biggs violently assaulted another train operator.

The operation was much like his life. Biggs was a petty criminal who was kicked out of the Royal Air Force and had already been in prison three times before the Great Train Robbery. He wasn't a particularly bright guy, but he was resourceful and wasn't afraid to use violence when necessary.

And, perhaps most importantly, Ronnie Biggs knew how to keep his mouth shut.

It wasn't Ronnie's mouth that got him busted in the Great Train Robbery, it was his fingerprint on a ketchup bottle recovered by the police at a farm the group used as a hideout. Biggs and eight of his accomplices were given thirty-year sentences and sent to the Wandsworth Prison.

Most people thought they had heard the last of Ronnie Biggs.

Prison, however, was nothing to Biggs but a chance to see some of his old mates and to devise his next move. Biggs carefully made a rope ladder and kept it hidden. When the time was right, he used it to scale the wall. He then made it across the English Channel to Paris, where his wife Charmian met him with his take from the Great Train Robbery. The couple then moved to Australia with their two sons and later had another son.

Life seemed good for Biggs in the late 1960s. The plastic surgery he got in France would surely throw the police off his scent, so he thought, and why would they look for him in Australia anyway?

Well, Biggs was wrong. Both he and his wife had maintained contact with friends and relatives in England, so it was probably one of them who eventually told the authorities Ronnie was in Australia. With the police closing in, Biggs made another big move.

Ronnie fled to Brazil in 1970 and had a child with a Brazilian woman, which prevented him from being extradited to England. He lived openly in Brazil for the next thirty years, visiting with tourists and giving interviews for fees. Ronnie Biggs had truly lived up to his name, but he never truly felt at home in Brazil.

He wanted to return to England to drink some English beer.

Ronnie returned to England in 2001 and was immediately placed back behind bars. His health deteriorated right away and he was hospitalized more than once. In August of 2009, just days before his eighty-first birthday, Ronnie Biggs was paroled on compassionate grounds.

Ronnie Biggs died on December 18, 2013, at the age of eighty-four, having lived enough in his lifetime for several people. But for those of you who may be foolish enough to try to duplicate Biggs' life, let his own words be a warning. When he looked back on his life on the run, he often did so with regret. In a statement from prison, he said:

"Even in Brazil I was a prisoner of my own making. There is no honour to being known as a Great Train Robber. My life has been wasted."

# Watch Where You Cut!

The circumcision of male children is ritually required in the Jewish religion and has become common among all religious communities in the United States over the last fifty years. The practice has its supporters and detractors: Supporters claim it is hygienic, while those against circumcision claim that the benefits are negligible and the procedure runs the risk of serious problems for the patient.

By "problems," I'm sure you can get the point!

This procedure predates the Jewish religion; it was first documented long before physicians knew about bacteria and germs or had the benefit of using anesthesia. A scene from the tomb of an Egyptian noble named Ankh-ma-hor, who lived during the reign of the King Teti (around 2345 BC), shows a man being circumcised in graphic detail. In the scenes, the man—whom scholars believe is actually the tomb owner's son—first has his "parts" prepared by a physician who shaves the pubic hairs. The second scene then shows the physician doing the deed.

But the physician needs an assistant to hold the arms of the man being circumcised!

It is important to point out a few things here, which the accompanying text sort of explains.

Above the preparation scene, the physician says: "I will make it comfortable."The patient then responds, "Rub it well in order that it may be effective."

It has been suggested that the patient is asking the physician to rub some sort of analgesic on his penis, but no effective pain reliever from the period is known today. This has led many modern scholars to suggest that the physician is talking about the cleansing process before the big cut happens. The scene on the left, which shows the actual cutting, is somewhat clearer.

As the physician cuts, he tells his assistant, "Hold him fast; do not let him fall!" The assistant responds, "I shall act for your praise."

The bottom text on the cutting scene has been the subject of some academic arguments, but the best translation of it seems to be: "Circumcising the hem-ka priest." Since Ankh-ma-hor was a vizier and not associated with any type of priesthood, it has been suggested that the man being circumcised in the scenes was actually one of his sons. The circumcision was part of his initiation into his cult/order, which is why it was taking place in adulthood.

Textual, artistic, and archaeological finds from other places and periods in ancient Egypt suggest that male circumcision was not universal and was possibly only reserved for the priesthood. Modern medical examinations of male mummies have shown that not all were circumcised and that it was done for nonmedical reasons.

But one thing is for sure about circumcision in ancient Egypt—it was nearly always done in postpuberty or adulthood... yikes!

# Oxen, Not Horses

Before the First Transcontinental Railroad was finished in America in 1869, pioneers in the 1840s and '60s who wanted to travel from the east to the newly developed territory of California had to do so on a "wagon train." The wagon trains were led by experienced frontiersmen and military veterans who knew the rugged west and often had some familiarity with the numerous Indian tribes and their languages.

If you wanted to take your family out to California, Utah, Oregon, or the southwest, the first thing you had to do was to get the supplies. You needed to buy a wagon, cooking supplies, guns for protection and hunting, and any tools you would need to fix your wagon. Some pioneers also brought along farming equipment or prospecting equipment, but those items were often available once they arrived at their destinations.

You would also need to buy some horses to pull your wagon, right?

Wrong. . .

In the mid-to-late 1800s, a horse or mule could cost ninety dollars, but an ox was about half that price. Oxen were tougher and more durable as well. So, most pioneers used these animals to pull their wagons and they would have their one family horse tied to the back. Or they would just buy a horse when they arrived at their destination. The entire cost (around one thousand dollars) was quite expensive for the time and represented life savings for most people.

After you bought your wagon, oxen, and supplies, you made your way to the Kansas City area to find a wagon master and a train. You paid the wagon master to lead you through the plains and mountains and also received his protection, as well as the protection of the rest of the train.

The organization and the numbers of the wagon trains meant that Indian attacks were rare, unlike what is shown in countless movies and TV shows.

Your biggest enemy would have been disease and the elements. If you or one of your family members got sick, you'd have to pray it would pass. If there was a major illness or injury, your only chance for survival was if there was a doctor on the train or you were near a town with a doctor. The elements were the real problem, though. If your train got caught in a blizzard in the Sierra Nevada Mountains, you might not make it out—at least not without eating some of the other people in your train, which is what happened with the Donner Party.

Once your train made it to the western edges of the Great Plains, you had a few options. You could go southwest on the Santa Fe Trail, into Utah on the Mormon Trail, northwest on the Oregon Trail, or continue west on the California Trail as most pioneers did. The entire trip could take up to six months one way.

So, the next time you hear about how horses helped tame the American west, remember that behind every graceful steed were a few slow, but reliable oxen.

# Knuckleballs

Today, Major League Baseball pitchers are known for their power, striking out batters with pitches that register around one hundred miles per hour. Sure, they throw the occasional curveball, slider, and changeup to keep the hitters guessing, but the majority of top pitchers rely on their fastball.

But this hasn't always been the case.

As the sport of baseball developed in the early twentieth century and evolved from a pastime into a major industry, pitchers devised different ways to get hitters out. Some pitchers who weren't capable of bringing in the "high heat" came up with different ways to grip the ball, which led to the curveball and "off-speed" pitches. Among these different pitches that were developed, one of the most storied is the knuckleball.

The knuckleball is thrown by digging the tips of the index finger, second finger, and thumb into the ball. This grip gives the pitch a much slower velocity—it only travels between sixty and seventy miles per hour—and makes it wildly unpredictable and difficult to hit.

Wild is the key word.

Catchers who catch for knuckleball pitchers generally have to use a much larger mitt; knuckleball pitchers routinely give up wild pitches and passed balls, which can allow runners on base to advance and, in some cases, let the batter take first base.

Considering the obvious problems associated with throwing the knuckleball, few have mastered the pitch, but there was once a "golden era of the knuckleballers." Jesse Haines perfected the pitch in the early 1900s and Hoyt Wilhelm followed suit in the middle of the century. Both players dominated the sport long enough to make it into the Major League Baseball Hall of Fame. But if you are reading this and know anything about the knuckleball, then you probably know about the Niekro brothers.

Phil Niekro and his younger brother Joe both had successful Major League careers from the 1960s through the 1980s: Phil amassed a lifetime 318-274 record and was inducted into the Hall of Fame, while Joe went 221-204. The brothers confused batters in both the American and National Leagues with their unpredictable knuckleballs; they even confused each other.

The Niekro brothers occasionally had to face each other in National League games as batters, and on May 29, 1976, Joe hit his only Major League homerun off his brother. Although Phil was the better pitcher statistically speaking, Joe gained more notoriety due to a humorous incident toward the end of his career.

During an August 1987 game when Joe Niekro was pitching for the Minnesota Twins at the California Angels' stadium, the umpire noticed that the ball had some strange scuff marks on it. Well, some old-school pitchers were known to doctor balls from time to time, especially knuckleball pitchers who relied on unpredictable ball movement. When the umpire asked Niekro to empty his pockets, he did so quite demonstrably to show the umpire and the stadium that he was an innocent man. But as Niekro waved his hands in a show of innocence, the file and sandpaper he was using on the ball fell out of his pockets. The umpire caught what transpired, as did all of America, as the scene was replayed on ESPN and local sports shows for the next week. The incident earned Joe a ten-game suspension but also an appearance on *Late Night with David Letterman*.

After the Niekro brother retired in the late 1980s, the knuckleball was seen less and less in Major League Baseball. Boston Red Sox pitcher Tim Wakefield was one of the last notable knuckleballers before he retired in 2011, and Boston currently has another successful knuckleball pitcher on its team, Steven Wright.

If you're a fan of the wily knuckleball, don't worry. Wright is only thirty-four. Since knuckleballers throw with far less velocity, they can pitch well into their forties, as the Niekro brothers did.

# Raise the Tally

You've no doubt heard or used the phrase "raise the tally" or "split the tally" plenty of times. Even if you don't know the origin of these terms, you can probably gather from the context that they have something to with accounting and are often money related.

A tally refers to a count, but it usually specifically refers to the count of something placed on a stick, which is known as a "tally stick." The person using the stick simply places marks on it, or tallies, which denotes the count of something. Beginning during the reign of King Henry I of England (1068-1135), the tally stick was used for tax purposes. As the shire sheriffs turned in their tax revenues to the royal Exchequer, marks (tallies) would be made on the stick denoting different amounts. The tally stick system was used until the early 1800s, when more modern accounting methods became easier and more practical to use.

Private individuals also used tally sticks to record economic transactions in medieval Europe.

If two parties made an economic transaction and there was a lack of hard currency available, the transaction would be tallied on a stick and then the stick would be split the long way so that both sides had a record. As the process became more accepted, a slight change was made by making the creditor's side of the tally stick a little longer, which meant that the debtor always got the "short end of the stick."

So, this explains *how* tally sticks were used, as well as the origin of some of the terms we still use today that are associated with economics. But when were tally sticks first used?

The funny thing about tally sticks is that they seem to transcend culture, language, and time. Tally sticks of one type or another have been discovered on every continent and from every historical period. The earliest known tally stick is believed to be a Paleolithic stick, over thirty thousand years old. It was discovered in central Europe and has fifty-five marks on it, which scholars believe was one of the first known tallies used by humanity.

But what would it have tallied? Perhaps Grog the caveman was keeping track of his wives, or the number of woolly mammoths he killed. There is no way to know for sure, but at least now you know what someone means when they say "split/raise the tally" or declares that they're getting the "short end of the stick."

# It's Always Sunny in Arica

In northern Chile and the extreme southern tip of Peru is the six-hundred-mile strip of land known as the Atacama Desert. It is by far the driest place on the planet, receiving less precipitation than even the polar regions. Very little grows in this desert and some areas can go decades without seeing any measurable rainfall.

Located right in the middle of the Atacama Desert, near Chile's borders with Peru and Bolivia, is the city of Arica. The city of Arica is a busy port city with over two hundred thousand inhabitants, and if you ever have the chance to visit, you are almost guaranteed to have a sunny stay. You see, Arica is the driest city in the world with an average rainfall of .03 inches.

Despite its lack of rainfall, Arica has a very pleasant climate. Average highs in the months of January, February, and March reach in the upper seventies Fahrenheit. (Chile is in the southern hemisphere so its seasons are the opposite from the north.) And, unlike other desert locales, the temperatures vary little throughout the year, which—along with the constant sun—has made it a popular tourist destination in recent years. Thousands of middle- and upper-class South Americans flock to the town to enjoy the sun, temperatures, and its fifteen-plus miles of nice beaches.

The waves in Arica are sweet too!

Surfers from the United States, Australia, Brazil, and Argentina have all traveled to the city to catch its tubular Chilean waves. The city has even hosted a number of professional surfing events.

But if you ever do make it to Arica, be sure not to wander too far from the city limits. Other than the main road that connects it to Bolivia, the roads in and out of the city are fairly primitive. If you break down in the Atacama Desert, it might be awhile before someone happens to come by, and you definitely can't count on rain for water.

# Not the Best Business Model

During the late 1970s and early '80s, Americans' love of all things kitsch combined with optimism for the year 2000 to create what was perhaps one of the most bizarre chapters in American pop culture and architectural history — the Xanadu houses.

You see, in the late 1970s, most of us were under the impression that by the year 2000, we would all either be dead from an apocalyptic nuclear war, or we'd all have robots and computers taking care of our every need. The American film industry made money in the 1980s by taking the first view of the future, while architect Bob Masters decided to take the more optimistic second route.

Masters truly was both an idealist and optimist and believed that affordable, automated homes could be built in the future. To demonstrate his theory to the world, he sprayed some polyurethane insulation over several balloons, creating a "house" in 1969. The invention didn't get much press, but it did attract the attention of Tom Gussel, who had the money to bankroll a much more ambitious business project. Gussel envisioned creating foam houses and equipping them with state-of-the-art computer technology. He believed, like Masters, that energy-efficient homes would be the wave of the future.

If only they could get people to see their idea.

Lucky for Masters and Gussel, they lived in America, the land where there is a very fine line between kitsch and tasteless. After scouting some potential locations for their invention, they decided to purchase some land in Wisconsin Dells, Wisconsin, which by 1979 was quickly becoming one of America's kitsch hot spots.

The pair decided to call their futuristic home Xanadu, after the medieval Mongol capital in China. What a thirteenth-century city had to do with a futuristic house was never explained, though.

Coincidentally, the film *Xanadu*, starring Olivia Newton John, was released in 1980. Well, it was a strange time and there is no doubt that Xanadu was a strange concept, although it proved to be very lucrative in its first few years. In fact, Xanadu was so popular that two more Xanadu home were opened in other American kitsch zones: Gatlinburg, Tennessee and Kissimmee, Florida.

Although ticket sales were good for all three locations, especially at the Florida home, the true intention was to sell Xanadu homes to private buyers. Another idealistic architect named Bob Mason designed the Kissimmee Xanadu home. He then planned to market similar homes to buyers for three hundred thousand dollars, with homes boasting less features for eighty thousand dollars.

Even in the 1980s, that was simply too much for most people.

Besides, by the late 1980s, technology was rapidly catching up and the Xanadu homes began to look real cheesy to most people. By the 1990s, home computers were more affordable, Windows was out, and the World Wide Web was becoming more widely used. The Wisconsin and Tennessee Xanadu homes were demolished in the early 1990s, but the Florida version continued for a few more years until it was shut down in 1996.

The Florida Xanadu home continued to serve as an unofficial weird attraction. By the early 2000s, people routinely took snapshots of the oddity and it became a destination for urban hikers and homeless people alike. Above all, the Florida Xanadu home became an eyesore to the city of Kissimmee, so the city leaders made the decision to finally have it demolished in 2005.

It may have seemed like a good idea at the time, but the Xanadu homes are proof that a business model that mixes kitsch and futurism just won't work.

# What Happened to My Cow?

Throughout the 1970s, a rash of bizarre incidents occurred in western states of the U.S. that involved the untimely deaths of cattle and other farm animals. Animals dying on farms is nothing new, but the manner in which they died was. These animals were often found with some of their organs removed, seemingly with medical instruments. They were also drained of nearly all their blood, without evidence of footprints (human or animal) in the area.

And sometimes, strange lights were witnessed in the skies over these scenes.

By the 2000s, thousands of these "cattle mutilations" (as they became known) had taken place, with the greatest number occurring in the 1970s in the states of Colorado and New Mexico. Though these freaky animal deaths remain unsolved, there are plenty of theories about them: natural decomposition, predators, satanic cults, covert government experiments, and alien experiments are among the most popular.

The first documented case of a cattle mutilation actually involved a horse. The King family were ranchers in southern Colorado who took great care of their livestock, so when they found their horse Lady dead in a field in 1967 they were quite surprised. Even more shocking was Lady's condition.

The flesh had been stripped from Lady's head, leaving the bone of her skull exposed. Several of her organs had also been removed with what appeared to be surgical precision, and there was very little blood left in the body.

Perhaps most perplexing was the fact that there were no human or animal footprints found anywhere near the corpse.

After Lady's strange death, other livestock mutilations began to appear across the west. In addition to the bizarre manner in which the animals were usually found, witnesses reported that wild and domestic animals, including flies, steered clear of the corpses. The victimized animals also often had their tongues, genital organs, and rectums removed. Laboratory examinations of some of these animals showed some anomalies, such as elevated levels of zinc and phosphorous, but nothing that pointed to any explanation.

But many have offered their own explanations.

The number of cases grew to the point that politicians from Colorado and New Mexico lobbied the federal government to do something. In 1979, an FBI investigation named "Operation Animal Mutilation" opened. The Bureau of Alcohol Tobacco and Firearms (ATF) also conducted an investigation, as well as the states of Colorado and New Mexico.

Each of the investigations consulted legitimate scientists as well as ranchers and farmers, most of whom came to the conclusion that the mutilations were the result of natural deaths and natural patterns of decay. For instance, the lack of blood was explained by the natural pooling of it, while the missing genital organs and rectums were explained by scavenging blowflies.

This probably explains many of the cases, but not all. Some of the mutilated cattle had *no* observable blood and many showed no signs of blowfly activity.

So, if many of these animals were killed by surgical precision, maybe it was the work of satanic cults?

This theory became popular in the wake of the Charles Manson Family murders. Other notable cults in the 1970s, such as Jim Jones' People's Temple, helped keep it alive. There were also two incidents in the fall of 1975 where groups of people wearing black robes were observed in rural Idaho, after which mutilated cattle were found in the area. Thanks to the "Satanic Panic" of the 1980s, belief in this theory continued into another decade.

But it would take a whole lot of cults to account for the thousands of mutilated livestock cases.

As is often the case with inexplicable events, UFOs and aliens became an explanation. In fairness to this theory, a number of respectable ranchers and farmers have claimed to have seen strange lights and unidentified flying objects moving in the skies above their mutilated life stock. The theory is that only alien technology could have made such precise incisions and that aliens are conducting some sort of experiments on our animals. In a number of these cases, "black helicopters" are seen along with the UFOs.

The black helicopter cases have led some to believe that the cattle mutilations are part of some major government conspiracy. The theory is that government has been experimenting on livestock as part of bioweapons programs. Advocates of this theory say that the presence of helicopters explains why there are often no footprints at the scenes of the mutilations. But it doesn't explain why the government, with all its vast resources, would need to experiment on random, privately owned livestock.

Finally, there are those who think the mutilations are the work of chupacabras. Remember them?

Although cattle mutilation is still reported from time to time, the number of cases has dramatically decreased since the 1980s. Maybe whoever was doing it got what they wanted.

# The Sailing Stones

Death Valley National Park in California and Nevada is known for its beautiful desert vistas, sand dunes, deep valleys, and extremely hot weather. It is also known for rocks that seemingly move on their own. These ambulatory rocks have been the subject of much debate and mystery, so much so that they have been named the "Sailing Stones."

The Sailing Stones can be found in a dry lake bed known as Racetrack Playa. They were first observed in the early 1900s by prospectors and other travelers who spent enough time in the lake bed to realize that a number of rocks, some of them quite large, were moving during the night. Word about the rocks began to spread and by the middle of the century a combination of curious onlookers, supernatural buffs, and legitimate scholars made their way to Racetrack Playa to see the phenomenon for themselves.

Everyone was surprised to see that rocks as big as humans sometimes moved hundreds of feet at night, in straight lines, curves, and even at right angles.

Few people could offer any explanation and no one ever actually saw the rocks move. But it wasn't long before people did start offering solutions to the mystery of what has become known as the Sailing Stones. Among the more reasonable-sounding explanations were gravitational and/or magnetic forces from the earth that were concentrated in the valley due to its salinity. Others thought that the winds coming into the valley were moving the rocks.

When those theories proved to be untrue, many thought the rocks were being moved by pranksters, but the park rangers pointed out that it would be difficult to do so since it was such a remote area of the park.

Of course, when all else fails, blame it on aliens!

Then, a number of scientists began noticing that the Sailing Stones only moved at night and during the winter when the desert can get fairly cold. Even under those conditions, the rocks only move about once every three years. By the 1970s, scientists began theorizing that the rocks were actually being moved by large, but thin ice sheets that melted when the sun rose —a process known as an ice shove.

In 2006, NASA scientist Ralph Lorenz decided to test this theory at home. According to Lorenz, he "took a small rock and put it in a piece of Tupperware, and filled it with water so there was an inch of water with a bit of the rock sticking out."

Lorenz then put the container in the freezer, and the rock consequently became embedded in a slab of ice. After taking the slab of ice out of the freezer, he gently blew on the rock, which moved it, leaving a trail. It seems that the Sailing Stones were moved by a combination of ice sheets on seasonal water blown by slight winds.

This theory was finally confirmed by GPS and time-lapse photography in late 2013 and early 2014. Recorded footage showed more than sixty rocks moving, some as far as seven hundred feet, in just a sixteen-minute span.

It seems the mystery of the Sailing Stones has finally been solved. But, as park ranger Alan van Valkenburg has said regarding park visitors who ask him about the rocks, "If you try to explain, they don't always want to hear the answers."

# Abraham Lincoln
# and Akhenaten

You might think the only thing that Abraham Lincoln, the sixteenth president of the United States of America, and the ancient Egyptian King Akhenaten (who ruled from 1351-1334 BC) had in common was the fact that they were both rulers. It is true that both men led their respective countries, exercised an incredible amount of influence on their people, and also left legacies that continue to this day. There is no doubt that both men were important rulers. However, there is also growing evidence that the men may have shared the same disease.

Lincoln's tall frame and long limbs led A.M. Gordon to suggest in an early 1960s volume of the *Journal of the American Medical Association* that the president was afflicted with a rare disease known as Marfan syndrome.

So, what are the details of this disease?

Marfan syndrome is a genetic disorder that affects the connective tissue. Those afflicted with the disorder will be tall, with disproportionately long, slender limbs, thin wrists, and long fingers and toes. Eye, heart, and lung problems are typical in Marfan syndrome cases. The common pathology of Marfan syndrome led Gordon, and then others, to conclude that Abraham Lincoln must have suffered from the disease.

After the treasures of King Tutankhamun's tomb were publicly displayed in traveling expeditions during the 1970s, interest in the pharaoh led to a renewed academic interest in his predecessor, Akhenaten. One of the first things a person notices when looking at either statues or paintings of Akhenaten are his bizarre and (some would say) ugly features. His bulb-shaped head is strange enough, but it is made even stranger as a result of his elongated hands, feet, and wide hips. His body seems especially disproportionate to Egyptologists when compared to artistic depictions of pharaohs from all other periods.

Some Egyptologists have looked to more esoteric answers for Akhenaten's unique artistic depiction, arguing that since he only worshipped one god, the Aten, his different body image was some sort of reflection of a new religious ideology.

Not every Egyptologist was convinced that the bizarre depictions of Akhenaten were symbolic, though, and many began looking to the medical field for answers. Eventually, A. Burridge and others noted that Akhenaten's features were indicative of Marfan's syndrome.

Unfortunately, we'll never be able to know for sure if Abraham Lincoln or Akhenaten suffered from Marfan's syndrome. But if you look at images of them side by side, you can definitely see some similarities.

# Disco's Dead

From the mid-1970s until the early '80s, the dominant style of popular music in America was disco. The style began in New York City and spread to larger urban centers on the coasts. By the late '70s, even Americans in small towns knew what the "hustle and bump" was, and disco themes were routine in movies and television shows of the period.

The legendary rock band KISS even made a heavily disco-influenced album, *Dynasty*, in 1979.

Disco's unique birth was a product of the times. On the one hand, the drug use and gay influence of the lifestyle associated with the music was a result of the 1960s counterculture. But the musical style itself was actually a protest against the music of that era—disco music was heavy on electronic beats and rhythms, as opposed to the traditional rock music of the counterculture.

Despite its quick ascent to the top of American pop culture, by 1982 it was safe to say "disco's dead." Actor Judge Reinhold even wore a shirt that said "Death before Disco" in the 1981 hit film *Stripes*.

So, what brought about this sudden—and at times violent—reaction to disco?

As with many other trends, disco became the victim of its own success. Interestingly enough, anti-disco sentiment came from both urban and nonurban segments of society. In the cities, the emergence of punk and new wave challenged disco on both style and content. Fans of punk and new wave craved a return to more a traditional and "do it yourself" type of music; furthermore, they viewed the attitude and lyrics of disco as vapid and superficial.

In Middle America, where bands like Lynyrd Skynyrd remained popular, the fad of disco quickly subsided and the heavy drug use and libertine sexuality often associated with the music were considered foreign. These somewhat disparate anti-disco groups coalesced to form a growing anti-disco attitude that was seen on T-shirts (as described above) and ironically in film and television. Though film and television had promoted disco in its early days, they were using the music style as a punching bag by 1980.

But if you could point to one particular date when disco began to die, it was July 12, 1979.

On that day, the Chicago White Sox were hosting their rivals, the Detroit Tigers, in a doubleheader at Comiskey Park. Anyone who showed up to the game with a disco record was admitted for the low price of ninety-eight cents as part of a promotion hosted by Chicago shock jock DJ Steve Dahl. Between the games, Dahl planned to oversee a controlled explosion of the disco records in a "Disco Demolition Night" event on the field.

Dahl set off the explosion and then all hell broke loose!

About seven thousand fans rushed the field, took bats and balls from the dugouts, tore the grass from the field, and ripped chairs out from the stadium. The Chicago Police riot squad came to the stadium about an hour later and made thirty-nine arrests. The White Sox were forced to forfeit the second game, but the true importance of the disco riot was the impact it had on American pop culture.

More than ten years before the World Wide Web came into existence, images of the Comiskey Park riot became viral on television screens across the nation and the idea of anti-disco riot became a meme. "Disco Sucks" T-shirts became popular with young people and, in short order, the culture changed.

Two years after the Comiskey Park riot, disco truly was dead.

# Snake Eyes and Dogs

Dice are one of the world's oldest types of games. Antecedents to dice have been discovered in ancient Egypt and India, but it was in Rome where people began to play it as we do today. It's really quite simple; you just place bets on which numbers will appear facing up after the dice are thrown. Although dice throwing is purely a game of chance, many people think they can control the results.

Don't tell them that the possibility of snake eyes, dogs, or boxcars happening is purely chance!

So, how did all those strange names become associated with different dice throws?

In most dice games, such as craps, a one on each die represents the lowest throw you can make. The two ones definitely look like eyes, but how they became associated with snakes probably goes back to the Bible. As dice throwing became more popular and rules were made within official gambling halls in the 1800s, the double ones began to be called "snake eyes"—probably because of the negative association of serpents with treachery. The Romans called it a "dog throw" for somewhat similar reasons.

Although the Romans kept dogs as pets (which is where the name "Fido" comes from), they often referred to people they didn't like or respect as dogs. As a result, a double one dice throw simply became known as a dog throw.

The opposite of snake eyes, double sixes, is usually referred to in dice games as "boxcars." The reasons for this term are a little murkier. Some gaming experts have said that the name is derived from the six's resemblance to a train's boxcar. But I'm not so sure.

Do you see it?

# That's Quite a Sunburn

The next time you're peering through a telescope, look between the constellations Libra and Sagittarius and you'll find the constellation Scorpius. It's sort of stuck in the middle of a bunch of other stars. Once you find it though, it might be difficult to make out the actual shape of a scorpion. I never see the shapes of those constellations. . . Oh well.

But more impressive than the constellation itself is one of its stars: Alpha Scorpii, which is more commonly known as "Antares." Antares is the brightest star in the Scorpius constellation and usually the fifteenth brightest star in the night sky, which is incredible because it is more than five hundred fifty light-years from our Sun! Antares (or, more precisely, Antares A) is part of a binary system, as it has a smaller brother star known as "Antares B." But since big brother literally outshines little brother, we really mean Antares A whenever we refer to Antares.

Antares is a red giant, which is the largest class of stars. And when I say large, I mean gargantuan. To put the size of Antares into perspective, let's consider the Sun. It is one hundred nine times larger than the Earth in diameter and it has an incredible three hundred thirty-three thousand times more mass. The Sun also accounts for about 98 percent of the mass of our solar system, which includes the big planets, although those are primarily made of gas.

So, we know the Sun is quite a bit bigger than our planet, but now I'm really going to blow your mind.

Antares has eighteen times the mass and eight hundred fifty times the diameter of the Sun. The star's red glow is sometimes so impressive that the ancient Greeks and Romans thought that it was the brother of Mars, which is how it got its name (Before Ares/Mars).

If you happen to be around in the next ten thousand years, you might even have the chance to watch Antares go supernova. When it does, it will be as bright as the moon at night and will be visible during the day.

But, it will probably give you the world's worst sunburn.

# Marky Mark and
# the Hate Crimes

You'd have to have been living in a cave (or on another planet) over the last twenty years if you don't know who actor Mark Wahlberg is. The forty-eight-year-old went from being a marginal musician in the early 1990s to an A-list actor by the end of the decade. Today, besides being one of Hollywood's top actors, he is a director and has his hands in a variety of different business and philanthropic ventures.

But "Marky Mark," as he was known during his brief music career, has a truly shady past.

Wahlberg grew up the youngest of nine children in south Boston. After his parents divorced in 1982, Mark spent most of his time living with his mother—and getting into trouble. He was close to his older brother Donnie and, as the two were bussed to different schools in Boston, they fell in with the wrong crowd. They began experimenting with drugs at a young age and joined a local white gang.

Donnie would go on to devote most of his time to his musical talents. Although Mark also showed promise in that regard, he spent most of his time doing and selling drugs and committing an occasional hate crime.

By the age of fourteen, Wahlberg had dropped out of school and had dedicated most of his time to being a local thug.

Wahlberg and his crew were known to have chased black kids out of their neighborhood on at least two different occasions, shouting racial slurs in the process. But the worst assaults took place in 1988.

On the night of April 8, 1988, Wahlberg was looking to get drunk. Since he was low on funds, he grabbed a five-foot-long stick and began looking for a mark. A short time later, he came across Thanh Lam walking down the sidewalk with two cases of beer. Wahlberg looked at the man and said "Vietnam fucking shit."

Wahlberg then hit Lam over the head with the stick, knocking him unconscious. The police quickly arrived on the scene, which sent Wahlberg fleeing on foot.

Desperate to avoid arrest, Marky Mark tried to solicit another man, Hoa Trinh, to hide him from the police. When Trinh refused, Wahlberg beat him. Marky Mark then tried to flee the area but was arrested not far from the scenes of the attacks. Initially, he was charged with attempted murder due to the serious injuries Trinh suffered—the victim was hospitalized and suffered permanent damage to one of his eyes. Because he had a good lawyer and was still a juvenile, Wahlberg was allowed to plead guilty to felony assault.

Though he was faced with the possibility of serving several years in a Massachusetts state prison, he only served forty-five days.

Years later, Wahlberg reflected on his life of crime.

"As soon as I began that life of crime, there was always a voice in my head telling me I was going to end up in jail. Three of my brothers had done time. My sister went to prison so many times I lost count. Finally I was there, locked up with the kind of guys I'd always wanted to be like. Now I'd earned my stripes and I was just like them and I realized it wasn't what I wanted at all. I'd ended up in the worst place I could possibly imagine and I never wanted to go back."

Luckily for Wahlberg, his older brother Donnie was well-connected in the entertainment industry as a member of the world-famous boy band, New Kids on the Block. (Mark was actually a member before they got famous, but his life of crime pulled him away from the group.) After meeting with agents and record producers, Mark Wahlberg was given a new image: Marky Mark, the bad boy white rapper who was still approachable to teenage suburban girls.

Wahlberg's career took off and most people forgot his past, at least until he applied for a pardon in 2014. When Marky Mark's crimes were made public once more, many people, including the woman who initially prosecuted him, questioned why he should be given a pardon.

Wahlberg withdrew his pardon application and publicly stated that he would never apply again.

# Don't Bother
# Exchanging Currencies

Those of you familiar with international travel know that exchanging your regular currency for the currency of the country you are traveling to is almost like a ritual. You either do so in the airport before you leave or after you arrive at your destination. The reality is that you really don't have to exchange your currency before you leave. Modern banking is more a matter of moving numbers around electronically than dealing with physical money. As long as there is an ATM machine around, you should be able to get your money.

But there aren't always ATM machines available.

And exchanging your currency is a ritual that is kind of fun. You look at the board to see the different exchange rates and then give the clerk your money. Within seconds, *voila*, you have a brand-new currency!

But if you're planning on taking a trip to Ecuador from the United States, don't bother exchanging your currency; they use the US dollar down there.

For most of its history, Ecuador used its own currency, the *sucre*. The country switched to the US dollar, however, after a financial collapse in the late 1990s. The move has helped to revitalize and stabilize Ecuador's economy and has made things much easier for American tourists and retirees. But, at the same time, it makes the fiercely independent Ecuadorans somewhat dependent on the United States. Unlike most nations that have their own currencies and can therefore move some decimal points in computers and/or physically print more cash, Ecuador needs to keep a steady stream of US dollars coming into its borders.

So, how have they been able to do this?

One of Ecuador's biggest exports is oil, which they sell in US dollars. Ecuador also receives millions in remittances from its citizens living overseas, as well as from tourists visiting their mountains, rainforests, and beaches. (Since going to the US dollar, Ecuador has become an increasingly attractive place for American retirees.)

Although the switch to the US dollar was initially opposed by a vast majority of Ecuadorans, the move has mostly been a success. "Dollarization"—as the switch to the dollar is referred to by economists—has brought Ecuador monetary discipline, severely reduced inflation, and has proven to be a boon for foreign investment.

Although some people in Ecuador have suggested bringing back their old currency, most experts don't believe that will happen anytime soon.

# Was It Really an Asp?

You don't have to be a historian to know who Cleopatra was, but here's a quick rundown anyway. Cleopatra was actually Cleopatra VII (who ruled from 51-30 BC), the Queen of Egypt and its sole ruler until the Romans conquered it in 30 BC. Cleopatra was part of the family known as the Ptolemies, Macedonian Greeks who ruled Egypt from 305-30 BC.

There's a lot to talk about with the Ptolemies, like how they institutionalized incestuous marriage. But we'll save that for another book!

For now, let's talk about how Cleopatra died. If you've seen the 1963 film *Cleopatra* (starring Elizabeth Taylor in the lead role) or the more recent series *Rome* on HBO, then you might think that Cleopatra died from a snake bite after her lover, Mark Antony, took his life in dramatic Roman fashion. Both of these are fictionalized accounts, but, like any good work of historical fiction, they are based on a fair amount of historical facts.

Based on the accounts of the Greek and Roman historians, we know that Mark Antony and Cleopatra fled to the palace in Alexandria, Egypt after losing the Battle of Actium to Octavian in 31 BC. We also know that Octavian led his forces to Egypt a few months later and that Mark Antony literally fell on his sword, as any good Roman solider would have done in a similar situation. We also know that Cleopatra died, but the details of her death are a little unclear, which perhaps adds more to her already alluring legend and personality.

Some of the fictionalized accounts have her trying to make a deal with Octavian that would have spared her life. When she realizes that the future Roman emperor is not going to listen, she lets an asp bite her. How much of that is true?

It is unknown if she tried to make a deal with Octavian, but it certainly wouldn't have been out of the realm of possibility. Cleopatra was shrewd—some would say conniving. It was truly a man's world, so the young queen had to be just as cold-blooded as the men she was around. After marrying her brother for political reasons, she later had him killed. She may have had a deep affection for Mark Antony, but she wouldn't have let her feelings for him get in the way of saving her own life. On the other hand, Octavian (who later changed his name to Augustus) was equally shrewd and would have had no use for a living Cleopatra, especially after he decided to make Egypt a Roman province. Octavian would have had Cleopatra brought back to Rome where she would have then been paraded in chains at a triumph dedicated to his victory. Afterwards, she would have been ritually strangled.

But what about that thing with the asp?

Well, the theory that she died from an asp began with the first-century BC Greek historian and geographer Strabo. In a passage about the history of the Roman Civil War, Strabo wrote:

"Augustus Caesar honoured this place because it was here that he conquered in battle those who came out against him with Antony; and when he had taken the city at the first onset, he forced Antony to put himself to death and Cleopatra came into his power alive; but a little later she too put herself to death secretly, while in prison, by the bite of an asp or (for two accounts are given) by applying a poisonous ointment; and the result was that the empire of the sons of Lagus, which had endured for many years, was dissolved."

So, the idea of death by snakebite was born, along with the theory of death by topical poison. Which one is correct?

The first-century AD Greek historian Plutarch echoed Strabo's account but added some more detail. He wrote that the asp was actually two cobras – a traditional symbol of Egyptian kingship – and that they were secretly delivered to the queen in a basket. The second-century AD Roman historian Cassius Dio also related the death by snakebite story.

So, it appears that this is one time when the movies actually do get it right.

# The Barefoot Bandit

Colton Harris Moore—born on March 22, 1991 in the seemingly quiet town of Mount Vernon, Washington—never had an easy life.

His parents divorced when he was very young and his stepfather died when he was seven. His father was not around much to provide Colton with a much-needed authority figure and he left the scene completely when Colton was twelve.

Colton's mother wasn't much better. She drank and often neglected her son, leaving him alone for days at a time. When she was around, Colton often acted out by breaking things, getting into fights at school, and running away from home. But despite his obvious problems, he displayed a brightness that most kids his age didn't have. Colton learned how to take care of himself on a daily basis and had a deep interest in different subjects. He was able to live on his own—even in the wilderness—for extended periods of time and had a mechanical aptitude that was unmatched for a teenager.

By the late 2000s, Colton had decided to go out into the wilds of Washington and become the Barefoot Bandit.

Colton began breaking into hunting and vacation cabins in Washington, Idaho, and British Columbia for food and supplies. He never really committed the crimes to make any money and rarely went after big-ticket items such as electronics. But, he would occasionally steal a car or truck to take him to his next score.

And then he started stealing airplanes.

Moore taught himself how to fly by reading books and researching on the Internet. For the most part, he was able to take off and fly without difficulty, but landing was another story. He tended to land his stolen planes like an albatross, which is how he caused the most damage. By late 2009, the authorities were on to Moore, who treated their search for him as a cat-and-mouse game. He sometimes left selfies on his victims' computers and once left bare footprints in chalk at one of his crime scenes, which is how he became known as the Barefoot Bandit.

With the heat on in the Pacific Northwest, Moore left the area in the summer of 2010, stealing cars all the way to Indiana. In Bloomington, Indiana, Moore then stole a Cessna 400 single-engine plane and decided to take some much needed R&R in the Bahamas.

After spending a couple of weeks in the Bahamas where his bare feet didn't stick out so much, Moore was arrested on July 11, 2010. Once he was returned to the United States, the Barefoot Bandit was charged with a litany of crimes in both federal court and Washington state court. He was eventually sentenced to seven-plus years in the Washington state prison system and six and a half in the federal system, but the sentences ran concurrently and he was released in July of 2016.

Since his release from prison, the Barefoot Bandit has kept a low profile, working as an office assistant for his lawyer.

Moore has said in interviews that his goal is to take proper flight training so that he can get his pilot's license. There is little doubt that Colton Moore will become a pilot if he sets his mind to it, and it is also likely that we haven't heard the last from him.

# Let's Meet up for Some Aggro Mate

The world of football hooliganism, or soccer as it's called in North America, is exotic and perplexing to people outside of countries where it is common. But in Europe, Latin America, and parts of Asia and Africa, violence by football team supporters has led to injuries, destruction of property, and even death.

And nowhere do they take their hooliganism more seriously than in England.

The sport of football/soccer began in England, so it should be no surprise that football hooliganism also first took root there when supporters of opposing teams began brawling with each other in the late 1800s. The violence increased until, after World War II, it became widespread and highly organized. Hooligans developed their own lingo by the late 1960s: hooligan gangs became known as "firms," the firms were composed of lads, and the lads were always looking for a little aggro (aggression).

And once a brawl starts, make sure not to get nicked (arrested) by the coppers.

The firm rivalries generally followed those of their teams' derbies (rivalries)—West Ham United and Millwall are among the most heated. The firms also have their own names.

For instance, West Ham hooligans are known as the Intercity Firm and the Millwall lads are called the Bushwackers.

By the 1970s, English hooligans became intertwined with the skinhead movement and the violence at matches was often uncontrollable. Riots were a regular occurrence, pitch invasions were frequent, and matches often had to be called. But the turning point came on May 25, 1985, when Liverpool FC fans went on a rampage in Heysel Stadium in Brussels, Belgium.

About an hour before a match between Liverpool and the Italian team Juventus, Liverpool hooligans stormed the Italian fans, causing a wall to collapse, which killed thirty-nine people. The violence led to dozens of arrests of English fans, a nearly six-year ban on all English teams playing outside of England, and an aggressive policy by British law enforcement to combat hooliganism.

For the most part, the law enforcement strategy has worked… in Britain.

British football matches are now peaceful, as the hooligans arrange their brawls outside of the stadiums and law enforcement has compiled extensive lists of known hooligans. But as the British clamped down on their hooligans, hooligans in other countries stepped up to try to win the title of most violent fans.

At the EURO 2016 in France, Russian hooligans were particularly active, invading a pitch and attacking English fans—hooligans and normal fans alike—on the streets. Russian ultras (as hooligans are often called outside of Britain) beat two English fans into comas after a match in Marseille.

I guess even football hooliganism has a way of coming around full circle.

# I Really Did See
# a Black Panther

If you live in North America, you've probably heard a story about someone seeing an elusive "black panther" somewhere. And by black panther, I don't mean the superhero movie that just came out or the black militants who carried guns and wore berets back in the 1960s.

No, I'm talking about a big cat with a black coat.

There have been sightings of these creatures in pretty much every state and even Canada. In fact, "black panthers" have also been sighted in England and Australia. But what exactly are they, and do they exist?

Well, the term "panther" is really just a generic term for any big, wild cat. It comes from the genus name *Panthera*, which includes lions, tigers, and jaguars. Of those species, jaguars are the only ones that are sometimes black, or melanistic, although even melanistic jaguars have spots that are visible up close. Cougars or Mountain Lions (genus *Puma*)—which are the only species of wild big cats in North America north of the Rio Grande—are not of the *Panthera* genus, nor do they have a gene for melanism.

So, what are the black panthers all of these people are seeing?

Since the nineteenth century, there have been numerous reports of "black panther" sightings across the United States.

"Panther" generally refers to a big cat, while most experts believe the black color seen by the witnesses is almost always a mistake.

Many experts believe that some of the black panthers sighted are actually melanistic ocelots—a small wildcat native to Mexico that occasionally wanders into the American southwest. That might explain some of the sightings, but it can't explain all of them, especially when there has been video documentation in some cases.

Some people who have claimed to have seen black panthers believe they are melanistic jaguars that have made it north of the Rio Grande, while others think they are a previously undiscovered subspecies of cougar. If these are an undiscovered species, this would make them a "cryptid." But skeptics are not so sure.

Skeptics believe that in the vast majority of cases the witnesses have in fact seen a cougar, but due to lighting and distance the animal appeared black. In the few cases where there is photographic evidence, skeptics point out that the size is often undetermined and the context of the film is questionable, so a proper judgement can't be made.

I guess that means that the elusive black panther will remain a legend until one is caught.

# The Real Life
# Robinson Crusoe

Many of you have probably read Daniel Defoe's 1719 novel *Robinson Crusoe*. If you haven't, then you've probably seen one of the numerous films and television shows based on the concept—an individual, or group of people, is stranded on an island for an extended period of time and must master the elements and their sanity to survive.

*Gilligan's Island* was a version of this story, so too was the 2000 Tom Hanks film, *Castaway*. And in case you're wondering: yes, the book *Swiss Family Robinson* was based on Defoe's work, which means that the cheesy-yet-lovable 1960s sci-fi television show *Lost in Space* also was.

If you have read *Robison Crusoe*, then you know it really isn't a kid's book: there is human trafficking, the slave trade, cannibals, and plenty of violence. And, as it turns out, it wasn't too far off from the real-life inspiration for the book—Alexander Selkirk.

Selkirk was born in 1676 in Scotland. From an early age, he was a problem for his family and the local community. He enjoyed fighting, stealing, chasing women, and causing havoc so much that he became a sailor when he was seventeen. He later became a privateer (a state-sanctioned pirate) for the British, which led him to the South Pacific in 1704, not far off the coast of what is today Chile.

When conflict between Selkirk and the captain came to a head, Selkirk's ship ended up on an uninhabited island on the Juan Fernandez archipelago in September of 1704. Selkirk argued that the ship was too damaged to sail and that he would rather stay on the island.

The captain obliged Selkirk.

Before leaving, Selkirk's captain gave him a gun, knife, hatchet, Bible, and various other provisions. Selkirk tried to change the captain's decision but to no avail.

Selkirk had the last laugh, however, as the ship did sink off the coast of what is now Colombia.

Selkirk moved into the island's interior and built a small shelter. He was able to live off a combination of fish, goats left by previous sailors, and berries, fruits, and other vegetables. He employed a couple of different techniques for contending with a large population of rats on the island. First, he made traps and placed them around his hut. Then he tamed the feral cats by feeding them during the day.

For entertainment and hope, he read his Bible, which gave him a new understanding of life.

He made clothes from goatskins and eventually had to make tools and weapons from branches, just as Gilligan and the crew did, well, sort of.

Selkirk's only companions were the feral cats, though he had a couple of encounters with sailors. But since the sailors were Spanish and he was a privateer for the British, Selkirk had to avoid them, or risk a possible execution or a prison sentence that would've been worse than his present situation.

Eventually, Selkirk was rescued in February of 1709 by British privateers.

But, just like a true pirate, Selkirk didn't let his marooning stop his activities. He went back to privateering and lived the rest of his life at sea until he died from yellow fever at age forty-five. Although Selkirk definitely lived an action-packed life, there is no evidence that he was involved in half of the things that Robinson Crusoe did in the book.

But I guess that's why it's called fiction, right?

# What Happened to
# Ambrose Bierce?

Ambrose Bierce was a true nineteenth-century American success story. Born in a log cabin in Ohio in 1842, Bierce grew up in Indiana and later served in the greatest conflict of his generation—the U.S. Civil War. Bierce's war experience left him with deep emotional scars, but it also gave him plenty of grist for his later writing career.

After the war, Bierce traveled around the country and to England before settling down to write for the *San Francisco Examiner*. While making a nice career for himself as a journalist, Bierce also wrote a number of fictional stories that were quite dark and bizarre for the time; they focused on the horrors of war and often contained supernatural subject matter.

But, like many writers, Ambrose Bierce was a tortured soul.

He struggled with his wartime experiences his entire life, and he experienced several tragedies while at the height of his success. He outlived both of his sons and he divorced his wife after learning that she was unfaithful. But the most interesting chapter of his life, which also happened to possibly be his last, took place when he left Washington, D.C. in October of 1913.

At the age of seventy-one and suffering from asthma, Bierce told his friends and family that he was going on a tour of Civil War battlefields he'd fought at. Although many thought the trip was macabre, they didn't consider it strange because they knew that Bierce was an eccentric person. No one heard from Bierce for months. Then a friend received a letter from him postmarked December 26, 1913 from Chihuahua, Mexico. According to the letter, he was traveling with Pancho Villa and his army, recording their campaign.

This is where things begin to get confusing.

Some later "witnesses" said that Bierce was either executed by Villa's men as a spy, or by the federales for being a revolutionary. His body was never recovered, and it should be pointed out that there is also no record of that December 26 letter.

There are plenty of other theories, some more believable than others.

One of the more plausible theories is that he committed suicide in a location where his body wouldn't be found. Bierce was an admirer of the Grand Canyon, so many think that his remains are there, although skeptics point out that millions of people have visited there in the subsequent one hundred years years and haven't found anything. With that said, the Grand Canyon is a big place and tourists only see a small fraction of it.

Some of the more bizarre theories have to do with Bierce continuing south from Mexico and being abducted and eaten by cannibal tribes in Central or South America. Since Bierce was an early sci-fi writer, some weird theories have him entering a portal into hell or another dimension.

Regardless of whatever happened to Ambrose Bierce, he would probably be happy to know that his disappearance created so much mystery. He'd also probably be wondering why no sci-fi writer has turned it into a story!

# Vulcan Blood

If you're a Trekkie, or even a casual follower of the Star Trek franchise, then you know that (along with his pointed ears) Spock was known for having green blood. If you don't happen to know what I'm talking about (don't worry, it just means you don't live in your mom's basement), Spock was a member of a fictional race of humanoids called Vulcans. The Vulcans' home planet was a dry, desert world, so they evolved in a way that gave them copper-based blood. This, in turn, gave it a green color.

As fantastical as the idea of green blood may sound, it is one of many strange but true science facts Star Trek creator Gene Roddenberry used for his writings.

If you are a user of the drug sumatriptan, you actually run the risk of your blood turning green. Sumatriptan—usually under the name-brand Imitrex—is most commonly used to treat migraine headaches. Without getting too technical, the drug works by blocking certain receptors. For most people, there are few side effects. But since sumatriptan contains sulfur, it can do funny things to your blood if you take too much of it.

Such as giving you *sulfhemoglobinemia*, which is just a nerdy way of saying green blood.

Sulfhemoglobinemia happens when sulfur atoms are integrated with hemoglobin molecules. Sulfide ions then combine with ferric ions to reduce the blood's ability to carry oxygen, which will turn a person's blood green and possibly lead to life-threatening consequences. In most known cases, the patient's condition improved and their blood went back to normal after the red blood cells naturally turned over. But, there is one interesting case from Canada.

In this particular instance, a middle-aged man fell asleep in a kneeling position, which caused "compartment syndrome," or an insufficient blood flow below his knees. When the doctor drew blood, as is standard, he was shocked to see that it was green! It was later discovered that the gentleman was suffering from sulfhemoglobinemia caused by an overdose of Imitrex.

His day started with a migraine and ended with green blood and surgery on his legs—poor guy.

# The Sky Samurai

Wars have a strange way of bringing out the best and worst in all of us. In every recorded war in human history, you can find great feats of heroism and sacrifice and extreme brutality and cruelty. Wars also have a way of bringing some truly interesting individuals to the forefront, people who would probably never be heard of otherwise.

World War II produced plenty of heroes, villains, and interesting individuals, one of the most interesting being a Japanese pilot named Saburō Sakai. Flying a Mitsubishi Zero, Sakai claimed between thirty and sixty aerial victories. He became well-known among American pilots, who respected the Japanese ace's skills, earning the nickname the "Sky Samurai."

But Sakai's story goes far beyond just being a war hero. Though he was a man who was never supposed to amount to much, the war gave him a chance to shine. The war also nearly took his life and left him questioning his role in the universe. Eventually, Sakai made peace with his former enemies and found his own meaning of life.

Sakai was born in Saga, Imperial Japan in 1916 to a distinguished family with samurai ancestry, which influenced him to pursue a career in the military. But things were never easy for him. The name he was given literally means "third son" in Japanese, which served as a constant reminder to him of where he rated in his family. His father died when he was just eleven, so he was sent to live with some relatives. His situation, however, didn't get much better.

Sakai did poorly in school and got into trouble. Then it was suggested to him that he should join the Imperial Japanese Navy.

Saburō Sakai found his place in the navy!

He became a pilot and quickly proved himself worthy by shooting down American plane after American plane. His fellow Japanese pilots respected him; the Americans both respected and feared him. Then came the Battle of Guadalcanal.

The Japanese knew that they had to stop the American advance at Guadalcanal, so it was all hands on deck. On August 8, 1942, Sakai and two other Japanese pilots came upon a group of American bombers over Guadalcanal and they decided to go in for an attack. After taking out two Grumman TBF Avengers, one of the tail gunners of another Avenger managed to shoot Sakai in the head. Somehow, Sakai was able to land his Zero on a Japanese airstrip and walk away from the plane.

Though he spent several months in a hospital, he was flying again in 1943. And he returned to active service in time for the Battle of Iwo Jima in 1944. Sakai was a hero in Japan. But, once Japan lost the war his fame quickly faded.

In the years immediately after the war, the Sky Samurai experienced another cycle of rough times. His first wife died, he had difficulty finding work, and he no doubt suffered from Post-traumatic Stress Disorder. Eventually, he found solace in the religion of his youth—Buddhism.

Sakai began to view the world in a Zen-like way and things began to slowly turn around. He held no ill will toward his former enemies. Nor did he feel anger or shame over the outcome of the war as some Japanese did, saying once in an interview, "Had I been ordered to bomb Seattle or Los Angeles in order to end the war, I wouldn't have hesitated. So I perfectly understand why the Americans bombed Nagasaki and Hiroshima."

One of the Sky Samurai's daughters eventually moved to the United States and he went there to visit, even meeting the man who had wounded him during the war, Harold Lew.

Sakai died in 2000 at the age of eighty-four, revered by some, admired by many, and respected by all.

# Pooing in Public

For people in industrialized countries, taking a dump is a very private affair. It doesn't matter if you're in North America where using toilet paper to clean yourself is the norm, or if you are in Europe, northeast Asia, or southern South America where bidets are more commonly used to clean up—pooing is done alone!

But this isn't the case everywhere. In numerous developing countries, such as India, many people live in places without proper sanitation and are therefore forced to poo in public. It isn't as much of a taboo to drop a deuce in public in these places as it is in industrialized countries, though having a private bathroom remains preferable.

But people haven't always thought this way. The ancient Romans, who are often considered among the most "modern" of all the ancient peoples, made going number two a communal experience. That's right, the same people who invented concrete, fire departments, and the world's first newspapers also had no problem pooing in public.

You may be aware that the Romans developed an extensive aqueduct system that brought running water into many of the elite's homes, and you may also know that they built extensive sewers under the streets of Rome. Often, what went into those sewers was human waste from one of the city's many public toilets.

By the fourth century AD, there were over one hundred forty public toilets—which were usually located next to the many public baths—scattered throughout Rome. The size of the public toilets could range from about ten pots to several times that amount. The toilets were pretty simple; they were basically just a series of open holes along a long bench where the men would sit to relieve themselves and talk to their fellow relievers or cacatori ("shitters"). The larger public toilets would sometimes have musicians to cover the bodily noises and baskets of fragrances to mask the putrid smell. Public toilets were something the Romans exported to the farthest reaches of their empire: from Britain to Turkey and all points in between, Roman public toilets have been excavated.

Of course, all Roman homes came equipped with facilities as well. The wealthy had toilets that emptied into the city's sewer system, while the less wealthy would have to use a commode/chamber pot. So, for many Roman men, taking a dump in public became something of a social occasion. It was a way to catch up on local news and maybe even make a business deal.

But the public toilets were strictly a man's world. Women were not allowed, and there were no "women only" public toilets.

The ladies had to wait until they got home.

# The Sweet Smell of Death

The phrase "the smell of death" probably brings the idea of decaying fish, mammals, or even people to mind. If you've had the unfortunate experience of smelling decaying flesh, then you know how strong and awful the odor is. Many describe it as a smell that literally stays with you for the rest of your life.

But not everything that dies emits a terrible smell. In fact, there is one type of death that actually smells very good and reminds everyone of summer.

It is the smell of grass being taken in the middle of its prime!

Most of you have smelled fresh-cut lawns in the middle of summer and probably enjoyed the scent. Not only is it a nice aroma, but it tends to bring to mind pleasant memories of our carefree childhoods and summer vacations. That smell comes to us thanks to an organic compound known as a green leaf volatile (GLV). GLVs are part of the natural defense systems of plants. Since plants can't fight or get up and run, they have evolved to handle threats quite a bit differently than animals. GLVs act differently in various plants and are often contingent upon the threat. For instance, when caterpillars eat coyote tobacco leaves they attract an insect that eats them!

Fortunately for us, no Mothra-sized creatures will come to our lawn's rescue when we cut it. Nonetheless, the smell the grass emits is a defense mechanism. But if it is a defense mechanism, why doesn't it actually seem act as a repellent, at least when it comes to humans?

It turns out that the GLVs grass emits when we cut it aren't the only GLVs that humans think smell good. Most fresh fruits and vegetables we eat also emit GLVs when they reach the end of their life cycles, which suggests that, just as plants have evolved by using GLVs for defensive purposes, humans have evolved to know when something is ripe and edible.

So, the next time you're taking a stroll through your local supermarket's produce aisle and enjoy the smell, just remember that it's the smell of death.

# The Song of Money

It's true that, in our modern society, money makes the world go round. We all need money just to survive and buy basic goods. Many of us make just enough to get by on, while others acquire more and more, passing it on to their family members.

We can say what we want about the current economic system, but the reality is that money is here to stay.

Even in communist regimes, such as the Soviet Union, which are supposed to eliminate greed and want, money has to be printed and minted. For modern countries, a barter economy isn't practical; a medium of exchange is needed to buy goods and pay taxes, which is why money came into existence. We talked about how coins became currency earlier in this book, so let's take a look at the first known example of paper currency.

You probably think that the Romans were the first people to use paper currency. Although that would be a good guess, you'd be off by several hundred years and several thousands of miles. The first examples of paper money were minted in the Song Dynasty (960-1279) of medieval China and, similar to the case in Lydia with coins, it was invented out of necessity.

During the Qin (221-206 BC) and Han (206 BC-AD 220) dynasties of China, one thousand round bronze coins with a square hole were threaded on a string as a full unit, or *guan*.

Though this could prove awkward if you needed to buy something that coast more than a thousand bronze coins, the system worked well until the early Song Dynasty. Besides the fact that carrying around strings of bronze coins could be cumbersome, it didn't really take into account the growth of the population and the economy.

And the Chinese economy was doing fairly well in the early Song Dynasty.

Under the "Green Sprouts Act" of 1069 (yes, that really is how the name of that law is translated from Chinese into English), the Song government offered farmers two state loans per year at the semiannual interest rate of 20 percent to be paid back with taxes. This deal was far more generous than private loans, which were usually given at 70 percent interest. So, many people took the government up on their offer.

Of course, this was long before checking accounts existed, so the government had to issue strings of coins.

I'm sure you can imagine what happened next. If not, you're about to get a crash course in macroeconomics and inflation.

By 1080, there were five million strings in circulation and the government was running low on bronze, so it decided to make the same fateful error the Romans had made about seven hundred years earlier—they added lead to the coins. Adding lead allowed the government to produce more coins, but it also devalued an already sinking currency. Prices went up and the Song government was facing a serious crisis. Luckily for the government though, the Song leaders valued learning, philosophy, and new ideas. A combination of advances in printing press technology and a new way of viewing the economy led the Song government to issue paper currency.

The first paper bill the Song issued was known as the *jiaozi*, but the longest lasting and most successful was the *huizi*. The *huizi* was first issued in 1160 with one bill equaling one string. The *huizi* was later backed by silver in order to prevent inflation, but overspending and printing led to the collapse of Song paper money in 1264.

It's no coincidence that the dynasty collapsed a short time later.

Although the Song Dynasty and its paper currency collapsed, the idea of paper money was in China to stay. The concept then spread throughout Asia, though it wasn't adopted in Europe until the late 1600s.

The funny thing is, despite the impact Song paper money had on the Asian world, not one bill has survived.

# "Yakety Sax"

There are few hit pop songs that nearly everyone knows without knowing the proper title. I mean, after all, most songs played on the radio say their title numerous times in the chorus, so it isn't too difficult to figure out the name. But, chances are you've heard the song "Yakety Sax" plenty of times in your life and you still don't know its name. Or, if you do, you refer to it as the *Benny Hill* song.

"Yakety Sax" was originally written by Americans James Q. "Spider" Rich and Boots Randolph and was performed by Randolph in 1963. For those of you who haven't heard the tune before, it's an instrumental that heavily features saxophones.

Both men were professional musicians who played in a number of different genres, but Randolph later made his mark in Nashville playing with some of Country music's biggest stars, including Elvis Pressley and Jerry Lee Lewis.

The idea for "Yakety Sax" is believed to have come from the sax solo in the popular 1958 doo-wop song "Yakety Yak" by the Coasters. Randolph recorded two versions of the song in 1960 and 1963, with it getting as high as seventy-nine on the Billboard 200, but it was quickly forgotten.

Until Benny Hill came along.

If you're a baby boomer or Gen Xer who grew up pretty much anywhere on planet Earth, then you've probably seen at least a few episodes of the *Benny Hill Show*. The British sketch comedy show, starring Benny Hill in nearly every skit, ran on television from 1955 to 1989. During its peak in the 1970s, it was broadcast to nearly one hundred countries. In the United States, episodes were often shown late at night on weekends on public television; the premium cable network HBO also showed unedited episodes.

The repeated sexual innuendos and double entendres on the *Benny Hill* may seem tame by today's standards, but they were truly risqué in the 1970s, and the *Benny Hill* show just wouldn't have been the *Benny Hill Show* without them.

The *Benny Hill Show* also wouldn't have been the *Benny Hill Show* without "Yakety Sax." The show began using its own version of the song performed by Ronnie Aldrich in its closing credits in 1969. As the credits would roll and the song would play, a silly accelerated chase sequence would take place, involving Hill and usually several scantily-clad young women. The international success of the show coincided with the addition of "Yakety Sax" in the concluding scenes.

I can say from experience that the closing credits sequence was extremely popular with young boys around the world!

In the decades since the *Benny Hill Show* has been off the air, "Yakety Sax" (or the "Benny Hill Show Theme" as many now know it) has been replicated along with the accelerated chase sequence. The song and sequence were famously used in the 2006 film *V for Vendetta* and have also appeared in numerous American animated television shows. There is little doubt that the catchiness of the tune and the slapstick nature of the *Benny Hill Show* will ensure the undying popularity of "Yakety Sax"/"The Benny Hill Theme."

# Did He Just Say That?

Let's face it, politicians all over the world are known for being duplicitous and corrupt, and for good reason: They often run on a platform to get elected and, once elected, either ignore their original ideas or change them to ones that are completely different. Once in office, many get involved in scandals that involve alcohol, drugs, women, sometimes men or boys, and (of course) payoffs.

But one thing that we can generally count on politicians to do is to say nothing of any value . . . usually.

During a June 28, 2016 speech to elected officials of the European Union, former Luxembourg Prime Minster and current President of the European Commission, Jean-Claude Juncker, spoke against BREXIT. He also seemed to say that he had recently been in communication with people from other planets. Yes, Juncker apparently claimed to be in contact with aliens.

Juncker delivered the speech in French, but here is part of the English translation.

"You need to know that those who observe us from afar are worried. I have seen, listened and heard many leaders of other planets and they are worried because they wonder about the course the EU will follow. So we have to reassure both the European [sic] and those who observe as from afar."

What was Juncker talking about? Is this evidence that the world's leaders know about the existence of extraterrestrials and they are keeping from us?

The official line is that Juncker merely made a mistake, a slip of the tongue, and that he meant to say "many leaders of our planet." This is actually quite easy to believe since he wasn't reading from a script. It should also be pointed out that Juncker is fluent in several languages and that he could have been a bit "off" or confused that day.

Most of Juncker's political opponents agree that the reference to people from other worlds was a slip of the tongue, but one that was alcohol induced. Juncker's political enemies like to point out that the Luxembourgish politician is a heavy drinker, although he himself denies those allegations. Most of the anti-Juncker crowd say that he just had one too many that day and said something silly while drunk. Why would aliens want to talk to him anyway, they add.

Still, conspiracy theorists and true believers in UFOs and alien life think it was a code he sent to the world wrapped in an average political speech. These people believe that Juncker's anti-BREXIT speech was actually a case of a politician practicing the rarity of speaking the truth. They believe that Juncker was attempting to prepare us for the imminent arrival of aliens.

I guess anything is possible—the existence of aliens and/or a politician speaking the truth.

# Droogs, Melchicks,
# and Devotchkas

"Ho, ho, ho! Well, if it isn't fat stinking billy goat Billy Boy in poison! How art thou, thou globby bottle of cheap, stinking chip oil? Come and get one in the yarbles, if ya have any yarbles, you eunuch jelly thou!"

If you've ever read the novel *A Clockwork Orange* by Anthony Burgess, or have seen the same-titled 1971 film starring Malcolm McDowell in the lead role, then you are familiar with the above quote. You might not understand everything it says, but you recognize its origin. For those of you not familiar with *A Clockwork Orange*, it is a novel about a dystopian future, where youth gangs run wild. The story is told by Alex, a gang leader who (although clearly psychopathic) has plenty of charisma. The complexities of the main character, along with a clever plot, are a couple of the reasons why *A Clockwork Orange* is considered a classic work of literature.

One of the other primary reasons for *A Clockwork Orange*'s success is its unique style and very unusual dialogue, which is known as *Nadsat*.

Like any good writer, Anthony Burgess wrote *A Clockwork Orange* based on some of his own experiences and observations, and he developed Nadsat through his extensive knowledge of several languages. He later said in interviews that since the book was sometime in the future in a world that was decaying from the inside, he wanted to invent an entirely new slang or vernacular that the youth gangs would use. Instead of using street vernacular from the early 1960s, he dove into his extensive knowledge of languages. He believed that by doing so, his book would never have a "dated" feel.

Most of the foreign words in Nadsat are Russian. In fact, the word Nadsat is Russian word for "teen." Along with the Russian words, there are also Romani and Cockney English words and phrases—Burgess was English and the book and film was set in England. Even the title of the book contained a Nadsat reference. "Clockwork" referred to the behavioral conditioning the government forced on the main character, while "Orange" was derived from the Malay word for "man."

The novel comes with a glossary, but you can pretty much figure out many of the words through context if you read the book or watch the film.

"Droog" is the Russian word for friend, which is one of the most common Nadsat words in the book and film. Following closely behind are the Russian words "melchick" (boy/young man) and "devotchka" (girl/young woman).

Some of the funniest-sounding words in Nadsat, though, are the Cockney terms. There is "baddiwad" (bad), "chumble" (mumble), "eggiwegs" (eggs), "pretty polly" (money), and one of the best ones, "pan handle" (erection).

In case you're still wondering about the opening quote, it's mainly just a bunch of non-Nadsat insults and gibberish with the exception of the word "yarbles," which is derived from the Russian word for "apples." You can probably guess what it means in Nadsat.

# Bombs Away!

Nature has come up with some pretty interesting ways for animals to defend themselves from other animals. Some animals have natural camouflage that allows them to blend in with their backgrounds, while others are fast or move in herds for protection.

Then, there is the bombardier beetle.

The bombardier beetle actually refers to any one of more than five hundred species of ground beetles that protects itself by shooting a boiling hot liquid chemical from its stomach that makes a popping sound. The bombardier beetles are of the *Carabidae* family and can surprisingly be found on every continent except Antarctica. So, chances are if you're reading this there could be one of these creatures in your area.

The way in which the bombardier beetle makes this unique explosion inside its body is not completely understood, although scientists know the basics. The explosion begins through a reaction when two different chemicals, hydroquinone and hydrogen peroxide, are combined into a weaponized mix. Thanks to modern photographic technology, scientists have watched this process happen. Each of the chemicals resides in a separate chamber in the beetle's abdomen until it encounters danger, at which point the two chemicals are mixed together until they reach a boiling point.

Then it can bomb its enemy.

The chemical is actually emitted from the beetle in a series of pulses, not a continual spray or a bomb as the name of the animal suggests. And the spray doesn't come out randomly either; the beetle can aim its weapon at its intended target. The weaponization of the spray is the result of it being both hot and corrosive: The temperature of the spray can get as high as 212°F with a corrosive effect.

You're probably wondering if bombardier beetles spray humans with this corrosive chemical? Yes, bombardier beetles commonly spray larger animals and humans when they feel threatened, but there is nothing you have to worry about. A spray attack from a bombardier beetle might burn for a little bit, but it will quickly go away. Actually, there is a good chance that you've been sprayed by a bombardier beetle and thought it was something else.

# Not the Mafia

The Sicilian Mafia, or Cosa Nostra, is well-known around the world through its fictional portrayal in books, film, and television. The *Godfather* movie trilogy (yes, even the last one) introduced millions of people to the arcane rituals and honor code of the Cosa Nostra, often portraying its members as sympathetic antiheroes. More recently, fans of the hit HBO show *The Sopranos* followed the lives of several mafia members as they tried to balance their often violent and always illegal work with home lives as upper-middle-class Americans in the 2000s. Despite the mafia originating in Sicily in the 1800s, it has become an American symbol in many ways: violent and amoral on the one hand, while also loyal and enterprising on the other.

But in Italy, the Cosa Nostra is not the only game in town.

Alongside the Cosa Nostra in southern Italy are two other notable crime syndicates: the Camorra and the 'Nadrangheta. Both of these organizations behave in much the same way as the Cosa Nostra. They engage in extortion, control smuggling in their regions, and run drug and prostitution rackets. These organizations also use violence to achieve their goals, emphasizing secrecy in their operations.

But the three organizations have different histories and structures.

The Camorra was first mentioned in a royal decree in the 1700s, but is thought to have originated in the 1600s in the Italian region of Campania, namely in the city of Naples. The Camorra existed for nearly two centuries as a collection of semiorganized thugs and hooligans. But it was transformed into a force to be reckoned with during the Italian independence movement of the mid-1800s. The pro-republican forces used the Camorra during some of the more violent street protests. By the late 1800s, the Camorra was one of the three major criminal syndicates and had expanded to countries with Italian diasporas around the globe.

The structure of the Camorra is horizontal in nature, with clans operating semi-autonomously. Despite not being tied to one leader or having a central structure, the Camorra clans live by a similar code that ties them together. The lack of a single leader has proven to be both beneficial and detrimental to the Camorra: The cell structure limits the effects that law enforcement raids have on the organization, but it also leaves the individual clans susceptible to other, larger criminal organizations.

Like the Camorra, the 'Ndrangheta historically operated in a horizontal structure; member clans were semi-autonomous but followed the same code. The 'Ndrangheta probably originated sometime in the mid-1800s in the region of Calabria, Italy, which put them physically between the Camorra and the Cosa Nostra. The 'Ndrangheta's proximity to the Camorra and Cosa Nostra has led to some conflicts with these syndicates, but there has mainly been cooperation among them—the leaders would usually come to agreements over territory and rackets.

But the decentralized nature of the 'Ndrangheta became problematic for it.

The various clans began fighting each other in the 1980s and 1990s, which resulted in hundreds of deaths and the syndicate assuming a more Mafia-like centralized structure. Once the smoke cleared, the 'Ndrangheta laid low while their Cosa Nostra counterparts fought with the Italian state. The result was the 'Ndrangheta's supremacy over the criminal underworld by the 2000s.

But in America, the Cosa Nostra is still king. The Camorra and 'Ndrangheta have both set up operations in the United States but, due to a combination of aggressive law enforcement investigations, the presence of other organized ethnic crime syndicates, and Cosa Nostra members' almost full integration into American culture (most know very little Italian), their members usually join American Cosa Nostra families.

Yes, the Camorra and 'Ndrangheta may be older and more powerful than the Cosa Nostra. But, due to the latter's "Americanness," it will continue to be the subject of many more Hollywood films as well as the premier Italian crime syndicate in the United States for years to come.

# About That Alien Abduction

Since the blockbuster film *Close Encounters of the Third Kind* came out in 1977, people around the world have been searching the skies for life of people outside our planet. In some ways, the movie gave the UFO movement a bit of legitimacy, as it was seen by many to be filled with kooks and crazies at the time. After the film's release, nearly everyone knew that a "Close Encounter of the Third Kind" meant actual contact with an alien.

Alien-human contact began to be discussed more earnestly on shows that featured paranormal themes such as *In Search of. . .* And people started to seriously consider that we might not be alone. Attention was given to some previous cases of alien sightings, with one in particular receiving significant consideration—the Allagash abductions.

In late August of 1976, brothers Jim and Jack Weiner and their friends Charles Foltz and Charles Rak were camping in the wilderness near Allagash, Maine, on the United States-Canada border. On the night of August 20, the four college students decided to go for a moonlit canoe trip in two separate canoes. Then, all hell broke loose.

The men left a large bonfire burning that could be seen for miles; presumably, it burned for several hours. The men claimed that, while they were at the middle of the lake, they saw a large shinning object hovering just over the tree line a few hundred yards in front of them. Foltz stated that he took a flashlight and flashed SOS to the object, which responded by shining a blue light on the two canoes. The men claim they then began furiously rowing back to their camp.

The next thing they remembered was being on shore. It was like they had lost a few minutes, no big deal. But when they looked at their bonfire, they noticed it was just smoldering coals.

Could they really have been gone for hours?

They left their campsite the next day and asked a park ranger about the lights. The ranger claimed that they were searchlights, so the men went home and basically forgot about the entire situation. The four of them went through college, got jobs and married, but kept in contact.

Then, twelve years later, Jim Weiner suffered a traumatic brain injury that left him with epilepsy and strange dreams about bizarre-looking little creatures doing experiments on him and his friends from the camping trip. Jim's doctors didn't believe him, but as he told more and more people about his story, he eventually met some people who seemed to have the answer.

They told Jim that it sounded like he and his friends had been abducted by aliens.

Jim and the others were put into contact with part-time hypnotist Anthony Constantino, who put all four men under for a session.

Under hypnosis, all four men claimed to have seen the same thing. The blue light beamed them onboard a spaceship where they were experimented on by "Gray aliens," who conducted medical experiments on them. Jack Wiener also had a mysterious growth removed from one of his legs that seemed to confirm the story.

It all seemed very good, perhaps a little too good.

The fact that all four related the *exact* same story began to raise suspicion. Witnesses to the same crime often see parts of it differently, and yet all four men seemed to have the same perspective of the incident. Others pointed out how unreliable hypnosis is and that Constantino was an English teacher by profession and a UFO enthusiast, making him far from objective.

Finally, as pressure over the case's validity began to mount, Rak claimed in a 2016 interview that the abduction claim was a hoax. Rak claims that the group did see something that night that could be classified as a UFO as they were fishing on Big Eagle Lake, but that the abduction never happened. He says that he never recalled anything about an abduction while under hypnosis; he and the others perpetrated the fraudulent story simply for monetary reasons.

"The reason I supported the story at first was because I wanted to make money," said Rak.

For their part, the other three men maintain that the abduction did happen.

# Mr. Hockey

Before Wayne Gretzky and Mario Lemieux became household names, Gordie Howe was the undisputed "King of Hockey." And he still is to most hardcore hockey fans. Howe was truly an iron man and player who epitomized an era that many remember with fondness—when goal scorers weren't afraid to get into fights and none of the players wore helmets. Howe really was a living legend. An anachronism on ice, he successfully played in a rare style, while all those around him tried to adapt to a flashier "made-for-TV" style of hockey. This is a big part of why he is such a towering figure in the sport.

Gordie Howe was born in 1928 in Saskatchewan, Canada and grew up during the Great Depression. He had to drop out of school to work, but he was signed to minor league hockey contracts by the mid-1940s. It didn't take Howe long to make it to the big time, moving up to play for the National Hockey League's Detroit Red Wings in 1946.

From that point on, number "9" would always be at the top levels of professional hockey.

After playing in the NHL for over twenty years, Howe, who was already in his forties, took his talents, and his two sons, to the upstart World Hockey Association (WHA). Howe was the WHA's MVP one season and is credited with bringing the new league legitimacy and viewers. He is also said to be one of the main reasons why some of the WHA merged with the NHL in 1979.

Howe finally ended his career in 1980 with the Harford Whalers—he was fifty-two and had played in five decades! Howe later played one game in 1997 for the Detroit Vipers of the International Hockey League.

Howe's list of hockey accolades is truly impressive. He led the NHL in scoring in six different seasons, won six Stanley Cups, and was awarded the MVP trophy in both the NHL and WHA. But perhaps the most impressive aspect of Howe's career was his resiliency and tenacity.

Today, goal scorers rarely fight and, in fact, fighting is somewhat now frowned upon. But things were much different in Gordie Howe's time, and some would say it was because of him. Besides never wearing a helmet (because real men don't wear helmets), Howe wasn't afraid to mix things up with the other team's goons. The opposing goons would often challenge Howe because he was a goal scorer and Howe was always happy to show them what a goal scorer could do with his fists.

Howe's combined prowess as a goal scorer and a fighter led to the coinage of the hockey phrase: the "Howe hat trick." Still in use today, the Howe hat trick is referred to when a player scores a goal, gets an assist, and gets into a fight.

Perhaps the most amazing part about Howe's career is how long he was not only able to play, but also to stay relevant. He was still scoring plenty of goals and breaking plenty of noses well into the 1970s when he was in his late forties. And professional hockey seasons are quite long—teams generally play about eighty games over a six-month span, not including the playoffs.

Needless to say, as one of North America's greatest sports heroes, Howe was a shoo-in for the NHL Hall of Fame and numerous other honors and awards in Canada and the United States. Unfortunately, Howe suffered from dementia late in his life, but he was cared for by his family who were with him when he died in 2016 at the age of eighty-eight.

# DON'T FORGET YOUR FREE BOOKS

# MORE BOOKS BY BILL O'NEILL

I hope you enjoyed this book and learned
something new. Please feel free to check out
some of my previous books on **Amazon**.